D1042049

The Greatest Question

The Greatest Question

by

Oliver B. Greene

The Gospel Hour, Inc., Oliver B. Greene, Director
P. O. Box 2024, Greenville, South Carolina

The Greatest Question

First printing, March 1966—10,000 copies
Second printing, July 1967—15,000 copies
Third printing, February 1969—15,000 copies
Fourth printing, January 1972—15,000 copies
Fifth printing, March 1974—15,000 copies
Sixth printing, November 1974—15,000 copies
Seventh printing, May 1976—15,000 copies

CONTENTS

CONTENTS

THE GREATEST QUESTION EVER ASKED

THE GREATEST QUESTION EVER ASKED

"Now at that feast the governor was wont to release unto the people a prisoner, whom they would. And they had then a notable prisoner, called Barabbas. Therefore when they were gathered together, Pilate said unto them, Whom will ye that I release unto you? Barabbas, or Jesus which is called Christ? For he knew that for envy they had delivered Him. When he was set down on the judgment seat, his wife sent unto him, saying, Have thou nothing to do with that just Man: for I have suffered many things this day in a dream because of Him. But the chief priests and elders persuaded the multitude that they should ask Barabbas, and destroy Jesus. The governor answered and said unto them, Whether of the twain will ye that I release unto you? They said, Barabbas. Pilate saith unto them, What shall I do then with Jesus which is called Christ? They all say unto him, Let Him be crucified. And the governor said, Why, what evil hath He done? But they cried out the more, saying, Let Him be crucified. When Pilate saw that he could prevail nothing, but that rather a tumult was made, he took water, and washed his hands before the multitude, saying, I am innocent of the blood of this just Person: see ye to it. Then answered all the people, and said, His blood be on us, and on our children" (Matt. 27:15—25).

The greatest question ever asked occurs in verse 22 of this passage: *"WHAT SHALL I DO THEN WITH JESUS, WHICH IS CALLED CHRIST?"* There are three reasons *why* this is the greatest question ever asked:

1. *It must be answered — it cannot be ignored.* Someone may say, "Mr. Greene, I would like to see you or anyone else make me answer that question! Could you force me to express myself concerning Jesus Christ? Could you make me talk if I shut my mouth and refused to open it?"

To *refuse* to open your mouth and confess the Lord Jesus Christ as the virgin-born Son of God, Saviour of sinners, would be saying in essence, "Away with Him! I do not want Him!" Actions speak louder than words, and you do not have to *say* anything to answer *that* question. There are *some* subjects on which you could be neutral. For example, if you were asked what church you belonged to, you could say, "I would rather not answer" — but that would not mean that you were not a church member. Or, if asked whether you are a Democrat or a Republican, you could ignore the question — but that would not mean that you were against either the Democrats OR the Republicans. You could refuse to answer either of those questions, thus professing neutrality; but to refuse to answer the question, "*Are you a Christian*? Do you love Jesus?" is to be against *Him*. Christ said, in Matthew 12:30: "He that is not with me is against me; and he that gathereth not with me scattereth abroad." The Psalmist declared, "Let the redeemed of the Lord say so" (Psa. 107:2). There is no such thing as neutrality concerning the Son of God. Either we gather people *to* Him, or we drive them *from* Him. Each day, by word or deed, we influence someone nearer to God, or drive someone closer to hell. God promises and warns simultaneously in Matthew 10:32,33: "Whosoever therefore shall confess me before men, him will I confess also before my Father which is in heaven. BUT whosoever shall *deny* me before men, him will I also deny before my Father which is in heaven." To refuse to confess God before men is to invite *Christ's* refusal to confess us before His heavenly Father.

Note this incident from the Word of God as recorded in Matthew 16:13—17:

"When Jesus came into the coasts of Caesarea Philippi, He asked His disciples, saying, Whom do men say that I the Son of man am? And they said, Some say that thou art John the Baptist: some, Elias; and others, Jeremias, or one of the prophets. He saith unto them, But whom say ye that I am? And Simon Peter answered and said, Thou art the Christ, the Son of the living God. And Jesus answered and said unto him, Blessed art thou, Simon Bar-jona: for flesh and blood hath not revealed it unto thee, but my Father which is in heaven."

On this occasion, some people thought that Jesus was Jeremiah, or Elijah, or John the Baptist, or one of the old prophets who had come back from the dead; but *Peter KNEW and CONFESSED* that Jesus was the Christ. Another time after Christ had preached a sermon on the bread of life and declared Himself to *be* that Bread, the people said, "This is a hard saying," and many of His followers turned back and walked with Him no more. Jesus then turned to His disciples and asked, "Will ye *also* go away?" Simon Peter answered Him, "Lord, *to whom shall we go*? Thou hast the words of eternal life. And we believe and are sure that thou art that Christ, the Son of the living God" (John 6:68, 69). Peter was convinced in his own heart that Jesus was the Christ of God. He believed it, and he *confessed* it.

Perhaps you are saying, "If I could *walk* with Jesus like Peter walked with Him, I too would believe and confess Him. It was easy for *Peter* to say, 'Thou art the Christ, the Son of God.' But I have never *seen* Jesus; I have never heard Him speak nor seen Him work a miracle. How can I know?"

The Word of God answers such an argument: "For I am not ashamed of the Gospel of Christ: for it is the power of God unto salvation to every one that believeth; to the Jew first, and also to the Greek. For therein is the righteousness of God revealed from faith to faith: as it is written, The just shall live by faith. For the wrath of God is revealed from heaven against all ungodliness and unrighteousness of men, who hold the truth in unrighteousness; because that which may be known of God is manifest in them; for God hath shewed it unto them. For the invisible things of Him from the creation of the world are clearly seen, being understood by the things that are made, even His eternal power and Godhead; *so that they are without excuse*" (Rom. 1:16–20).

There is no excuse for any person, including the heathen, to ignore or deny the existence of God. The things of God are manifest in creation, and even the *invisible* things of God can be understood through that which IS visible. David said: "The heavens declare the glory of God; and the firmament sheweth His handywork. Day unto day uttereth speech, and night unto night sheweth knowledge. There is no speech or language, where their voice is not heard. Their line is gone out through all the earth, and their words to the end of the world. In them hath He set a tabernacle for the sun" (Psa. 19:1–4). Anyone who will look up into the starry heavens knows there *must* be a Supreme Being who controls all nature and the vast solar systems of this earth. Certainly the people in *America* are without excuse, because the Gospel has been preached in every city and town, every hamlet and community in this land. The Word of God is simple—it is clear and plain, and *anyone* can have access to a Bible in order to read the story of Jesus.

Everyone MUST answer the question Pilate asked the Jews: "*What shall I do then with Jesus, who is called Christ?*" No one can be neutral. The Jews who brought Jesus before Pilate said, "Crucify Him! Crucify Him! Let His blood be on us and on our children." Almighty God gave them exactly what they asked for concerning their children. No group on the face of this earth has suffered such a deluge of blood as has the Jew! No person can read the history of the Jewish people and then deny the fact of the *inspiration* of God's Word.

2. *This question must be answered NOW.* The answers to other questions can be postponed—but to refuse to answer "What shall I do with Jesus?" is to declare that you are definitely NOT a believer in the virgin-born Son of God. Furthermore, to refuse to answer the question NOW may mean an eternity in hell. God deals in the *eternal present.* He who has been *from* everlasting and who will be *through* everlasting (Psa. 90:1,2) does not deal in the future concerning salvation. Solomon put it this way: "Boast not thyself of tomorrow; for thou knowest not what a day may bring forth" (Prov. 27:1). Paul said, *"Now* is the accepted time; behold, now is the day of salvation" (II Cor. 6:2).

"Boast not thyself of tomorrow . . . Now is the time . . . Today is the day of salvation." *"What shall I do then with Jesus who is called Christ?"* MUST be answered now, because we have no promise of the next sixty seconds! And even if we *had* the assurance that we would live another day, another month, another year, the Bible plainly states that no man knows the day or the hour wherein the Son of God will come back to this earth. That means He could return *this* day, this hour, this very moment; and anyone not prepared for His return will be without any hope of salvation whatsoever. (Read II Thessalonians 2:1–12.)

Some years ago a dear old gentleman asked me to come talk with him about his soul. He died during the course of our conversation, although he was apparently as healthy as any person I have ever seen when I arrived at his home. He asked me this question: "What did you say the other

morning about being born again? What is the new birth?"
After turning to John chapter three in my Bible and reading
the first five verses, I paused to explain the new birth; and
when I lifted my eyes from my Bible, the old gentleman was
dead! The last words that man said were: "Mr. Greene,
what did you say about being born again?"

On another occasion, a young man sat in one of my
meetings. He was unsaved, and when I asked him to come
to Jesus he said, "Preacher, when I get *ready* to be saved,
I will *be* saved. You will not need to come for me, I will
come forward myself." The next morning that young man
suffered a severe heart attack and was unconscious until
the next day. When he regained consciousness, his pastor
and I instructed him from the Word of God in the plan of
salvation, and he prayed an unforgettable prayer: "God,
be merciful to me a sinner. Forgive me my sins, come into
my heart and save me! Lord, I am sorry I put it off until
You seemingly struck me down . . . but Lord, have mercy
on me and save me!" He had regained consciousness just
long enough to trust Jesus, then dropped into a coma and
died.

But no one can depend on a death-bed repentance.
Death often comes too quickly or too unexpectedly for that.
"*Today* is the day of salvation. *Now* is the accepted time.
Seek ye the Lord while He may be found; call upon Him
while He is near!"

Listen to this tremendous passage from God's Word:

"How long, ye simple ones, will ye love simplicity?
And the scorners delight in their scorning, and fools hate
knowledge? Turn you at my reproof: behold, I will pour
out my spirit unto you, I will make known my words unto
you. Because I have called, and ye refused; I have stretched
out my hand, and no man regarded; but ye have set at nought
all my counsel, and would none of my reproof: I also will

laugh at your calamity; I will mock when your fear cometh; when your fear cometh as desolation, and your destruction cometh as a whirlwind; when distress and anguish cometh upon you. Then shall they call upon me, but I will not answer; they shall seek me early, but they shall not find me; for that they hated knowledge, and did not choose the fear of the Lord: They would none of my counsel; they despised all my reproof. Therefore shall they eat of the fruit of their own way, and be filled with their own devices. For the turning away of the simple shall slay them, and the prosperity of fools shall destroy them. But whoso hearkeneth unto me shall dwell safely, and shall be quiet from fear of evil'' (Prov. 1:22—33).

Notice God said that because He had called and they refused, because He had stretched out His hand and they did not regard it, because they had set at nought all of His counsel and would not listen to His reproof, He would *therefore* laugh at their calamity and mock when their fear came. When they called in their distress, He would refuse to answer. And because they had despised His reproof, He promised that they would "eat the fruit of their own way and be filled with their own devices." There will be a multitude of people at whose calamity God will laugh. He will laugh when they call, beg, and seek His face. They will eat the fruit of their own way, for they will have had their chance and will have refused it—the Bible is very clear about that. They will reap what they have sown. The most dangerous thing anyone can do is to hear the Word of God and then refuse to believe it. No one can be neutral concerning Jesus, and it is spiritual suicide to put off the answer to the all-important question, "What shall I do with Jesus who is called Christ?"

3. *The answer to this question determines not only where*

we spend eternity but also *what we are on this earth.* The health we enjoy, the friends we have, the job we operate, the society in which we live, the money we have are all greatly influenced by whether we are saved or lost. The answer we give to this all-important question touches every minute detail of life here on this earth. A sin committed many, many years ago can cause suffering and heartache for the rest of one's life.

Parents should *get their children converted as early as possible,* for the answer to the question, "What shall I do with Jesus?" will determine to a great extent the success of those children in every avenue of their lives.

The answer to this greatest of all questions will settle your eternal destiny. To answer the question with "I believe He is the virgin-born Son of God; I believe in the death, burial, and resurrection of the Son of God, the Lord Jesus Christ, and I trust Him now as my personal Saviour!" is to have everlasting life.

The question is NOT "Do you live a good life?" Or "Are you doing the very best you can?" Or "Are you sincere in your religion?" Or "Do you support the church with your presence and your money?" God's Word says: "Not by works of righteousness which we have done, but according to His mercy He saved us, by the washing of regeneration, and renewing of the Holy Ghost" (Titus 3:5). Again, "For by grace are ye saved through faith; and that not of yourselves: it is the gift of God: Not of works, lest any man should boast" (Eph. 2:8,9).

Salvation, therefore, is not attained by good living, liberal giving, or good works. "There is therefore now no condemnation to them which are *in Christ Jesus . . .*" (Rom. 8:1). Christ IS salvation — "*Christ in you,* the hope of glory" (Col. 1:27). God promised that "as many as re-

16

ceived Him, to them gave He power to become the sons of God, even to them that believe on His name: which were born, not of blood, nor of the will of the flesh, nor of the will of man, but of God" (John 1:12,13). The way you answer this greatest of questions will determine your eternal destiny.

In closing, hear the Word of God once more: ". . . if thou shalt confess with thy mouth the Lord Jesus, and shalt believe in thine heart that God hath raised Him from the dead, thou shalt be saved" (Rom. 10:9). That is the verse that opened the door of heaven for me and brought salvation to my soul. I confessed the Lord Jesus, I believed in my heart that He was crucified, buried, and that God raised Him from the dead. I did what the verse told me to do, and God kept His Word! He saved me, I KNOW I am saved, and I have *enjoyed* my salvation from that moment until this very hour! Romans 10:9 gives the two essentials for salvation: *confession* with the mouth, and *belief* in the heart. God said it, and He cannot lie. "*Whosoever* shall call upon the name of the Lord shall be saved" (Rom. 10:13).

What is *your* answer to the question, "What then shall I do with Jesus who is called Christ"? You cannot be neutral; you must answer that question—*and do it NOW*. And remember—your answer will determine where you spend the ceaseless ages of eternity!

FOUR QUESTIONS
YOU MUST ANSWER BEFORE GOD

FOUR QUESTIONS
YOU MUST ANSWER BEFORE GOD

The Bible records four questions God asked which no man can afford to ignore. The first of these is found in the third chapter of Genesis:

The First Question God Ever Asked Man

This is the second question in the Word of God, the devil having asked the first one; and the way Eve answered the *devil's* question made it necessary for God to ask HIS first question of man. In his question to Eve, the devil implied that God had not been fair when He told her and Adam not to eat of the fruit of the tree of the knowledge of good and evil. Eve listened to Satan, she sinned, and thereby she lost her perfect estate with God. Not satisfied with her *own* disobedience, she tempted her husband and he also sinned. When the two of them had eaten of the forbidden fruit and realized that they were naked, they did what all sinners since then have tried to do: They sought their own means of restoration. They made fig leaf aprons in an attempt to cover their shame.

Although the garments Eve made for herself and Adam might have been beautiful in *their* eyes, there was something drastically wrong with them; for even though they had covered their nakedness, Adam and Eve still hid among the trees of the garden — proof beyond doubt that they had a guilty conscience, something that the fig leaves would not cover. *They knew they had disobeyed God* and they feared His displeasure!

Up until the day they sinned, these parents of the human race had waited with glad anticipation for God to visit them each day in the cool of the evening; but on this day when God came down to visit them they were nowhere to be seen. God then asked the first question ever asked of man: *"Adam . . . WHERE ART THOU?"* (Gen. 3:9).

Hiding among the trees of Eden, Adam was lost and in need of a Friend — but he was hiding from that Friend, the One who had given him everything he had, even life itself. Instead of hiding, he should have been calling, *"God, O God! Where are YOU? I NEED YOU! I have sinned, I have disobeyed you. Please forgive me and come to my rescue!"*

Adam's *answer* to God's question is recorded in Genesis 3:10: He said, "I heard thy voice in the garden, and I was afraid, because I was naked; and I hid myself." Adam had never before been frightened at the voice of God, but now he knew that he had *disobeyed* his Creator, and thus he *feared*.

When God asked Adam how he had found out he was naked, he tried to lay the blame on Eve: "The woman whom thou gavest to be with me, she gave me of the tree, and I did eat." But that strategy did not work for Adam — and it will not work for sinners today. It was Adam's own fault that he had failed. God had told him plainly and specifically what to do and what *not* to do; *but he purposely and deliberately disobeyed.*

We are reminded of the words of James when, under inspiration of the Holy Spirit, he wrote, "Let no man say when he is tempted, I am tempted of God: for God cannot be tempted with evil, neither tempteth He any man: *But every man is tempted, when he is drawn away of his own lust, and enticed.* Then when lust hath conceived, it bringeth forth sin: and sin, when it is finished, bringeth forth death" (James 1:13–15).

God's question to Adam has significance for us today.

22

We are either children of God or children of the devil — that is, we are sinners, or we are sons of God. We are headed either for heaven or for hell. To all the world today God is calling, "*Where art thou*?" He seeks the souls of men and calls for them to come to Him for rest, just as Jesus invited when He was on earth, "Come unto me, all ye that labour and are heavy laden, and I will give you rest" (Matt. 11:28).

The First Question God Ever Asked of Woman

This question is recorded in Genesis 3:13: "And the Lord God said unto the woman, *What is this that thou hast done*?"

You will notice that when the Lord God found Adam and Eve hiding among the trees of Eden, He asked *Adam* how he knew that he was naked. Why did He ask Adam instead of Eve? The answer is simple: God had given Adam authority over every other living thing, and had also made him head of the human family. Because woman is the weaker vessel, it was *Adam's* responsibility to keep the home together and see that God's instructions were carried out.

Then when the Lord had finished with Adam He turned to Eve and asked of her, "What is this that thou hast done?" Even though Adam was head of the house, Eve had to give account of her own sin. She could not shift her sin to Adam any more than *we* can shift *our* sins to our parents or friends. Each person must give an account for *himself*: "For we must all appear before the judgment seat of Christ; that every one may receive the things done in his body, according to that he hath done, whether it be good or bad" (II Cor. 5:10).

But poor Eve followed Adam's example and tried to

23

shift the blame to someone else. She said, *"The serpent beguiled me, and I did eat."* Adam laid the blame on his wife, Eve laid it on the serpent, the serpent said nothing — but all of them paid for their own sin.

At the time the serpent came to Eve he was not the loathsome, repulsive thing that he is today. He was one of God's most beautiful creatures; but because he allowed Satan to enter into him and tempt Eve to sin, God cursed him: *"Because thou hast done this*, thou art cursed above all cattle, and above every beast of the field; upon thy belly shalt thou go, and dust shalt thou eat all the days of thy life"* (Gen. 3:14).

"What hast thou done, Eve?" She did not know it then, but she had sold the entire human race into sin, into death and suffering. Every tear that falls today is the result of the sin of Eve. There would be no suffering and sorrow today had Eve not yielded to Satan. What a price woman has paid because of Eve's sin! God said to her, "I will greatly multiply thy sorrow and thy conception; in sorrow thou shalt bring forth children; and thy desire shall be to thy husband, and he shall rule over thee"(Gen. 3:16).

And what a price *Adam* paid for listening to his wife, instead of listening to God! God had told him what to do and what not to do, but he followed the wishes of his wife instead of following Divine instruction, and God had no choice but to place him under the curse: "Because thou hast hearkened unto the voice of thy wife, and hast eaten of the tree, of which I commanded thee, saying, Thou shalt not eat of it: cursed is the ground for thy sake; in sorrow shalt thou eat of it all the days of thy life; thorns also and thistles shall it bring forth to thee; and thou shalt eat the herb of the field; in the sweat of thy face shalt thou eat bread, till thou return unto the ground; for out of it wast

24

thou taken: for dust thou art, and unto dust shalt thou return'' (Gen. 3:17—19).

God cursed the serpent, He cursed the woman, He cursed the man—and He cursed the ground! ''Eve, what is this thou hast done?'' She thought it a little thing to take a bite of the one fruit God had told Adam not to eat — *but see the tragic, far-reaching results*! There are no ''little'' sins in God's sight. It took the precious blood of His dear Son to atone for even the least of all sins!

''Eve, WHAT HAST THOU DONE?'' Had Eve followed God's instructions, that question would never have been asked; but because she did not obey God, she turned from the fountain of life to the fountain of death. Because she introduced sin and disobedience into the world, rivers of tears have been shed and blood has flowed from that day until this present hour. During Eve's lifetime she saw what a terrible thing her disobedience has brought upon mankind. She lived to see one of her sons kill his brother, all because of sin. Had Eve not sinned, neither Cain nor Abel would have had to bring a sin offering, and therefore no argument could have arisen over the sacrifices they brought to God.

The Question God Asked Cain

Genesis 4:9 records God's question to Cain: ''And the Lord said unto Cain, *Where is Abel thy brother*?'' Cain was angry because God had accepted Abel's offering and had rejected *his*. But Abel had followed God's instructions and had given the firstlings of his flock, whereas Cain, like the modernists of today, did not want to bring a ''bloody sacrifice.'' It is evident that he saw no need for God's plan of the shedding of blood for an atonement. He carried an offering according to his own fancy — and God rejected it!

25

This made Cain angry, and later, when he and Abel were in the field, "Cain rose up against Abel his brother, and slew him." One sin unrepented always calls for another. God paid Cain a visit and asked him a question: "Where is Abel thy brother?" Cain replied, "*I KNOW NOT. Am I my brother's keeper?*" He had just committed first degree murder—*and now he was lying about it!* He lied to God, and he paid dearly for it. God said, ". . . The voice of thy brother's blood crieth unto me from the ground. And now art thou cursed from the earth, which hath opened her mouth to receive thy brother's blood from thy hand; when thou tillest the ground, it shall not henceforth yield unto thee her strength; a fugitive and a vagabond shalt thou be in the earth. *And Cain said unto the Lord, MY PUNISHMENT IS GREATER THAN I CAN BEAR!*" (Gen. 4:10–13).

I would ask all fellow Christians this question: "*Where is THY brother?*" The vast majority of Christians today think nothing of the masses who are going to hell all around them. Few Christians even take the time and trouble to invite their neighbors and lost loved ones to church, or attempt to show them the way to God. Some say, "I do not believe in *persuading* people"—but PAUL believed in persuading them! King Agrippa said, "Paul, *almost* thou *persuadest ME* to be a Christian." In II Corinthians 5:11 Paul said, "*Knowing therefore the terror of the Lord, WE PERSUADE MEN . . . .*"

"*Where IS thy brother?*" ARE we our brothers' keeper? Christ's mission on earth was singular: *He came to seek and to save that which was lost* (Luke 19:10). He said to His disciples, ". . . Pray ye therefore the Lord of the harvest, that He would send forth labourers into His harvest" (Luke 10:2). In the parable of the "ninety and nine" (Luke 15:4–7), the shepherd did not rest until he had found the one lost sheep. When the prodigal son returned home there was feasting and merry-making over his return — but there was no rejoicing during his absence from home, while he abode in the "far country" (Luke 15:11–32).

Paul said, "If our Gospel be hid, it is hid to them that are lost: in whom the god of this world hath blinded the minds of them which believe not, lest the light of the glorious Gospel of Christ, who is the image of God, should shine unto them" (II Cor. 4:3,4).

"And you hath He quickened, who were dead in trespasses and sins" (Eph. 2:1).

"When I say unto the wicked, Thou shalt surely die; and thou givest him not warning, nor speakest to warn the wicked from his wicked way, to save his life; the same wicked man shall die in his iniquity; but his blood will I require at thine hand. Yet if thou warn the wicked, and he turn not from his wickedness, nor from his wicked way, he shall die in his iniquity; but *thou hast delivered thy soul*" (Ezek. 3:18,19).

Hear this question again: *"AM I MY BROTHER'S KEEPER?"* James 5:20 replies: *"Let him know, that he which converteth the sinner from the error of his way shall save a soul from death, and shall hide a multitude of sins!"* Yes, we ARE our brothers' keeper.

The Question God Asked Elijah

In I Kings 19:9 God said to Elijah, *"What doest thou here, Elijah?"* That great prophet was running from Jezebel; he had gone into the desert to live the life of a hermit, because the wicked queen had threatened his life. He who had been a giant for God had become a spiritual coward and was hiding in fear for his life. Elijah, who up to this hour had been one of God's greatest prophets, had

27

taken his eyes away from God and could see nothing but Jezebel and her threat to his safety; and he now sat under a juniper tree, wishing himself dead.

But God found him there, and in essence said to him, "Elijah, what in the world are you doing here in the desert under this old juniper tree, discouraged, despondent, and wishing for death? Those who need your message are back in the city and throughout the countryside. Elijah, you have left the flock to the mercy of wolves—the worshippers of Baal are tearing down my altars and rebuilding their own. Where are the prayers and vows you made at Carmel? Have you so soon forgotten what you saw and experienced there? Do you not know that the God who delivered you at Carmel can deliver you again? Do you not know that your God is mightier than the wicked Ahab and Jezebel? Why are you afraid? Elijah, *what doest thou here*?"

Elijah ran from the opportunity of a lifetime when his eyes focussed on a wicked queen instead of upon God. In this there is a principle involved for every Christian in every Age. A Christian out of place and out of God's will is not only the most *miserable* of creatures, he is also a stumbling block. The devil can use a careless, disobedient Christian to greater degree than he can use a drunk in the gutter! If Satan can make a Christian miserable, take away the joy of his salvation, and make him a spiritual coward, that Christian then becomes a stumbling block in the way of sinners.

Now let us apply these four important questions to the Christian life:

"*Where art thou*" in relation to your salvation? Are you running away from God? Or are you trying to hide behind church membership and "religion"? If this be true, just remember that you cannot hide from God: "The eyes

28

of the Lord are in every place, beholding the evil and the good" (Prov. 15:3). "Neither is there salvation in any other: for there is none other name under heaven given among men, whereby we must be saved" (Acts 4:12).

"*What hast thou done?*" Are you in the will of God? Are your works the works of righteousness? Does your daily life give strength to the weaker children of God? or do your deeds cause the weaker brethren to stumble? What have you done for Christ? If you are doing nothing, or if you are doing but little, wake up and go after the lost for Jesus!

"The fruit of the righteous is a tree of life; *and he that winneth souls is wise*" (Prov. 11:30). "*And they that be WISE shall shine as the brightness of the firmament; and they that turn many to righteousness as the stars for ever and ever*" (Dan. 12:3).

"*Where is THY brother?*" What are you doing to lead him to the Lamb of God who taketh away the sin of the world? We ARE our brother's keeper, whether we like it or not; and if we do not accept that responsibility, we will have to give an account at the judgment bar of God. Again I remind you of the solemn declaration that "we must all appear before the judgment seat of Christ; that every one may receive the things done in his body, according to that he hath done, whether it be good or bad" (II Cor. 5:10).

"*What doest thou here?*" Are you out of fellowship with the Lord? Are you living a consecrated life —or are you living in the world for a few moments of worldly pleasure? Do not be like poor Elijah, running away from the "Jezebels" of our day. God has a remedy for spiritual cowardice:

"Wherefore take unto you the whole armour of God, that ye may be able to withstand in the evil day, *and having done all, to stand.* STAND therefore, having your loins girt about with truth, and having on the breastplate of righteousness; and your feet shod with the preparation of the Gospel of peace; above all, taking the shield of faith, wherewith ye shall be able to quench all the fiery darts of the wicked. And take the helmet of salvation, and the sword of the Spirit, which is the Word of God'' (Eph. 6: 13–17).

May God's Holy Spirit bring to salvation those who need Christ as Saviour. May He help all Christians to do what He would have them do; and above all, may we be faithful and true in our stand for Him, ready to render service when He needs us to do something for Him!

"TO WHOM SHALL WE GO?"

"TO WHOM SHALL WE GO?"

"Verily, verily, I say unto you, He that believeth on me hath everlasting life. I am that bread of life. Your fathers did eat manna in the wilderness, and are dead. This is the bread which cometh down from heaven, that a man may eat thereof, and not die. I am the living bread which came down from heaven: if any man eat of this bread, he shall live for ever: and the bread that I will give is my flesh, which I will give for the life of the world.

"The Jews therefore strove among themselves, saying, How can this man give us His flesh to eat? Then Jesus said unto them, Verily, verily, I say unto you, Except ye eat the flesh of the Son of man, and drink His blood, ye have no life in you. Whoso eateth my flesh, and drinketh my blood, hath eternal life; and I will raise him up at the last day. For my flesh is meat indeed, and my blood is drink indeed. He that eateth my flesh, and drinketh my blood, dwelleth in me, and I in him. As the living Father hath sent me, and I live by the Father: so he that eateth me, even he shall live by me. This is that bread which came down from heaven: not as your fathers did eat manna, and are dead: he that eateth of this bread shall live for ever.

"These things said He in the synagogue, as He taught in Capernaum. Many therefore of His disciples, when they heard this, said, This is an hard saying; who can hear it? When Jesus knew in Himself that His disciples murmured at it, He said unto them, Doth this offend you? What and if ye shall see the Son of man ascend up where He was before? It is the spirit that quickeneth; the flesh profiteth nothing: the words that I speak unto you, they are spirit, and they are life. But there are some of you that believe not. For Jesus knew from the beginning who they were that believed not, and who should betray Him. And He said, Therefore said I unto you, that no man can come unto me, except it were given unto him of my Father.

"From that time many of His disciples went back, and

33

walked no more with Him. Then said Jesus unto the twelve, Will ye also go away?

"Then Simon Peter answered Him, *Lord, to whom shall we go? Thou hast the words of eternal life.* And we believe and are sure that thou art that Christ, the Son of living God.

"Jesus answered them, Have not I chosen you twelve, and one of you is a devil? He spake of Judas Iscariot the son of Simon: for he it was that should betray Him, being one of the twelve" (John 6:47—71).

The sixth chapter of the Gospel of John contains the great discourse on the bread of life. Jesus reminded the Jews that their fathers ate manna in the wilderness — but their fathers died. Then He clearly stated, *"I am the LIVING bread which came down from heaven: if any man eat of THIS bread, he shall live for ever*: and the bread that I will give is my flesh, which I will give for the life of the world."

The Jews could not understand this saying; they did not know what He was talking about, and when Jesus said to them, "Except ye eat the flesh of the Son of man, and drink His blood, ye have no life in you," they murmured among themselves saying, "This is an hard saying; who can hear it?"—and from that moment on, *"many of His disciples went back, and walked no more with Him."* (When God's man today preaches God's Word in all of its purity and power, he is accused of preaching a "hard Gospel."

Jesus said, "The *words* that I speak unto you, they are spirit and they are life." In other words, eating the flesh of the Son of God and drinking His blood is simply appropriating the Word of God, assimilating the Word of God by faith. "In the beginning was the WORD, and the Word was with God, and the Word was God. . . *And the Word was made flesh*, and dwelt among us . . ." (John 1:1,14). Jesus was

34

that flesh. Thus, when we *hear, receive,* and *appropriate* the Word, we are eating the flesh and drinking the blood of the Son of God. The Word of God is *alive;* it is the seed through which life comes.

When many turned back from following Him, Jesus then turned to the twelve and asked, *"Will ye ALSO go away?"* It was Simon Peter who answered, *"LORD, TO WHOM SHALL WE GO? Thou hast the words of eternal life. And we believe and are sure that thou art that Christ, the Son of the living God!"*

Peter was convinced that Jesus was the Son of God and that through the words He spoke — and ONLY through those words — eternal life could be his.

To Whom Shall YOU Go?

Are *you* saved? Are you *born again* through faith in the finished work of Jesus? If you are not, then I ask you, "To whom *shall* you go?" Jesus alone has the words of eternal life!

I offer a few of the things to which people are going today, things upon which they are relying to get into the kingdom of God:

1. Living a good life:

One of the outstanding errors today is the teaching that if we live a good life, practice the "golden rule," and do the very best we can, that is all God requires of us. Those who hold to this belief are following a false hope — but let the Word of God explain it:

"And when (Jesus) was gone forth into the way, there came one running, and kneeled to Him, and asked Him, Good Master, what shall I do that I may inherit eternal life? And Jesus said unto him, Why callest thou me good? There is none good but one, that is, God. Thou knowest the commandments, Do not commit adultery, Do not kill, Do not steal, Do not bear false witness, Defraud not, Honour thy father and mother. And he answered and said unto Him, Master, all these have I observed from my youth. Then Jesus beholding him loved him, and said unto him, One thing thou lackest: go thy way, sell whatsoever thou hast, and give to the poor, and thou shalt have treasure in heaven: and come, take up the cross, and follow me. And he was sad at that saying, and went away grieved: for he had great possessions" (Mark 10:17—22).

This young man was in a hurry — he came *running*; and the fact that he *knelt* before Jesus tells us that he came in the spirit of humility. He asked, "Good Master, what shall I do that I may inherit eternal life?"

Jesus, knowing all things, knew that this young man believed Him to be a great teacher, a great healer, a worker of great miracles; but He also knew that the boy did not believe Him to be the Son of God. Therefore He asked, "Why callest thou me '*good*'? There is none good but one, that is, GOD."

In other words, Jesus said to this young ruler, "Young man, if I am *good*, then I am GOD; and if I am *not* God, then I am not GOOD, for there is no one good but God."

This boy was religious, he was a student of the Old Testament Scriptures. Jesus said to him, "You know the commandments" — and notice the commandments He named:

> "Do not commit adultery.
>
> Do not kill.
>
> Do not steal.
>
> Do not bear false witness.
>
> Defraud not.
>
> Honour thy father and mother."

36

Not one of these commandments mentions Deity. Jesus named the commandments having to do with our fellowman, not those having to do with our relationship to God. *Adultery* is a sin against a fellowman; *stealing*, *lying*, and *defrauding* are sins against our fellowman; and the same is true of the other commandments mentioned here.

But notice the young man's reply when Jesus named these commandments: He said, *"Master, all these have I observed from my youth!"* Jesus knew this boy's heart, and yet He did not contradict him; He did not say, "You are not telling the truth"—so there is a possibility that he HAD kept the commandments named. It is not *probable*, but it is possible. Looking upon him, Jesus loved him and said to him, *"One thing thou lackest*: Go thy way, sell whatsoever thou hast, and give to the poor, and thou shalt have treasure in heaven: and come, take up the cross, and follow me."

Jesus did not quote the *first* commandment, "Thou shalt have no other gods before me," for this young man *already* had a god: he was in love with his houses and lands! Jesus offered him a paid vacation for the rest of his natural life, and treasure in heaven throughout eternity. He offered to relieve him of all of his financial worries and the anxiety that goes along with owning and caring for property. He simply said to the boy, "If you want everlasting life, sell your property and trust me. I will give you treasures in heaven." But the Scripture tells us that *"he was sad at that saying, and went away grieved: for he had great possessions."*

If this young man had believed that Jesus was God in flesh, he would have believed His promise; but he considered Jesus as only a great teacher, a great man; he did not believe that He was the Son of God. He had lived a good, clean moral life, he had practiced the "golden rule"; but he lacked one thing—the one thing every unbeliever lacks: *faith in the Lord Jesus Christ.* Unbelief sent him away with a sad heart. John 3:18 tells us, "He that believeth on Him (Jesus) is not condemned: but he that believeth not is condemned already, *because he hath not believed in the name of the only begotten Son of God.*" Every soul that burns in hell today is there because of the sin of unbelief; and if you, dear reader, are so unfortunate as to spend eternity in the lake of fire it will be because you refused to believe on Jesus and commit your soul to Him!

"For by grace are ye saved through faith; and that not of yourselves: it is the gift of God: not of works, lest any man should boast" (Eph. 2:8,9).

Are YOU depending on good living to get you to heaven? If you are, you are in grave error. Jesus spoke a parable concerning those who trust in good living; it is recorded in Luke 18:9—14:

"And He spake this parable unto certain which trusted in themselves that they were righteous, and despised others:

"Two men went up into the temple to pray; the one a Pharisee, and the other a publican. The Pharisee stood and prayed thus with himself: God, I thank thee, that I am not as other men are, extortioners, unjust, adulterers, or even as this publican. I fast twice in the week, I give tithes of all that I possess.

"And the publican, standing afar off, would not lift up so much as his eyes unto heaven, but smote upon his breast, saying, God be merciful to me a sinner.

"I tell you, this man went down to his house justified rather than the other: for every one that exalteth himself shall be abased; and he that humbleth himself shall be exalted."

The "religious" man in this parable had a good record

insofar as good living is concerned; few of us could measure up to such a record. By contrast, the publican would not even lift his eyes toward heaven where God dwells. He smote his breast (denoting humility and a contrite heart) and prayed, *"God be merciful to me a sinner!"* Only seven words — but notice that the publican recognized God, confessed that God is a God of mercy, confessed that he himself was a sinner, and asked God to be merciful to him *because* he was a sinner. He did not claim to be good, he made no claim to having lived a good life. He simply confessed that he was a sinner and called on God for mercy. That is the only prayer God will *hear* from an unbeliever.

But notice also that Jesus said this man went home *justified*—not the Pharisee, the man whose life was so "upright," but the poor, sinful publican. He closed the parable with the warning that "every one that exalteth himself shall be abased; and he that humbleth himself shall be exalted."

No, good living is not enough to get us to heaven. It took the best heaven had—the sinless, spotless, holy Son of God—to pay the sin-debt. He was the righteousness of God, the holiness of God, *in flesh*, tempted in all points as we are, yet without sin. He was that sacrificial Lamb without spot or blemish, and He laid His life down that WE might have life through faith in His finished work. The only way any sinner can be saved is by receiving the Lord Jesus Christ and trusting in His shed blood.

2. *Doing good works:*

There are those who are trusting in their good works to get them to heaven. Writing to Titus, Paul said: "For we ourselves also were sometimes foolish, disobedient, deceived, serving divers lusts and pleasures, living in malice and envy, hateful, and hating one another. But after that the kindness and love of God our Saviour toward man appeared, *not by works of righteousness which we have done, but according to His mercy He saved us, by the washing of regeneration, and renewing of the Holy Ghost; which He shed on us abundantly through Jesus Christ our Saviour*; that being justified by His grace, we should be made heirs according to the hope of eternal life" (Tit. 3:3–7).

"Works of righteousness"—right doing, right living—will never save anyone. According to Isaiah 64:6, *"We are all as an unclean thing, and all our righteousnesses are as filthy rags*; and we all do fade as a leaf; and our iniquities, like the wind, have taken us away." It was JESUS who lived a spotless life. HE worked the works of God that we might be *saved by grace apart from works.*

"Where is boasting then? It is excluded. By what law? of works? Nay: but by the law of faith. *Therefore we conclude that a man is justified by faith WITHOUT THE DEEDS OF THE LAW"* (Rom. 3:27,28). Regardless of how many good works you may do, regardless of how righteous your life may be, good works and righteous living can never save you. Jesus said, "Not every one that saith unto me, Lord, Lord, shall enter into the kingdom of heaven; but he that doeth the will of my Father which is in heaven. Many will say to me in that day, Lord, Lord, have we not prophesied in thy name? and in thy name have cast out devils? and in thy name done many wonderful works? And then will I profess unto them, I never knew you: depart from me, ye that work iniquity" (Matt. 7:21–23).

To whom then will you go? Not to good works or righteous living. Put your faith and trust in Jesus, who paid the sin-debt on Calvary. God grant that you not be one of the "many" who will say in that day, "Lord, we have done good works, we have preached and taught and lived, we have been righteous," only to hear Jesus say, "Depart from me, I never knew you! You did not do my will, you did not put your faith in my shed blood!"

3. Baptism:

There are tens of thousands of church members today who have gone into the baptistry, thinking that baptism saves; but that is not according to the teaching of God's Word. We *should* be baptized in water, in the name of the Father, Son, and Holy Ghost—but only because we *are* saved, not in order to BE saved. Baptism is for believers. An *unbeliever* cannot be baptized in the true sense of the word; he can be put under the water, but that is not Christian, baptism.

Baptism denotes death, burial, and resurrection—death to sin; we are buried with Christ, we are raised to walk in newness of life; but baptism does not save us nor does it help to save us. Water baptism is in obedience to the command of Jesus; it is an outward expression of an inward possession, an outward testimony that we have died to sin and the world and that we are raised to live a new life in Christ Jesus.

One may go into the baptistry and come out to live the same old life; but those who are *baptized into Christ* by the Holy Spirit live a NEW life: "For by one Spirit are we all baptized into one body, whether we be Jews or Gentiles, whether we be bond or free; and have been all made to drink into one Spirit. . . Therefore if any man be in Christ, he is a new creature: old things are passed away; behold, all things are become new" (I Cor. 12:13; II Cor. 5:17).

41

This Is the Message

"This then is the message which we have heard of Him, and declare unto you, that God is light, and in Him is no darkness at all. If we say that we have fellowship with Him, and walk in darkness, we lie, and do not the truth: But if we walk in the light, as He is in the light, we have fellowship one with another, and the blood of Jesus Christ His Son cleanseth us from all sin" (I John 1:5–7).

The atoning blood is a *sin-remover*: "For then must (Christ) often have suffered since the foundation of the world: but now once in the end of the world hath He appeared to put away sin by the sacrifice of Himself" (Heb. 9:26).

The atoning blood *heals the conscience*: "For the law having a shadow of good things to come, and not the very image of the things, can never with those sacrifices which they offered year by year continually make the comers thereunto perfect. For then would they not have ceased to be offered? because that the worshippers once purged should have had no more conscience of sins. But in those sacrifices there is a remembrance again made of sins every year. For it is not possible that the blood of bulls and of goats should take away sins" (Heb. 10:1–4).

The atoning blood *provides victory for the believer*: "And they overcame him by the blood of the Lamb, and by the word of their testimony; and they loved not their lives unto the death" (Rev. 12:11).

The atoning blood *brings blessings to the believer*: "The cup of blessing which we bless, is it not the communion of the blood of Christ? The bread which we break, is it not the communion of the body of Christ?" (I Cor. 10:16).

42

The atoning blood *crucifies self*: "I am crucified with Christ: nevertheless I live; yet not I, but Christ liveth in me: and the life which I now live in the flesh I live by the faith of the Son of God, who loved me, and gave Himself for me" (Gal. 2:20).

The atoning blood *separates us from the world*: "Wherefore Jesus also, that He might sanctify the people with His own blood, suffered without the gate. Let us go forth therefore unto Him without the camp, bearing His reproach" (Heb. 13:12,13).

The atoning blood is a *love-inspirer*: "For the love of Christ constraineth us; because we thus judge, that if one died for all, then were all dead: and that He died for all, that they which live should not henceforth live unto themselves, but unto Him which died for them, and rose again" (II Cor. 5:14,15).

To be cleansed by the precious blood of Jesus means more than having the pimples of the world and the blotches of sin removed from the face of life; it means *purification of the heart's affection*. To be cleansed by the blood of Christ means that the bad blood which *caused* the pimples and blotches is removed and *new* blood takes its place. Therefore believers are new creatures in Christ Jesus. We live a new life and we walk in a new path—in the straight and narrow way.

To whom then shall we go? Shall we go to good living? Shall we trust in good works? Shall we trust in our own righteousness? or in giving money? or in sacrificing "things"? Shall we go to the baptistry to find peace and eternal life? Not one of these things—nor all of them combined—can satisfy the human heart. Jesus is the only One who can give eternal life; there is no other. God grant that you realize here and now that apart from Jesus you are hopelessly and eternally lost. It *must* be "Christ in you, the hope of glory" (Col. 1:27).

WORDS

Peter asked Jesus, "Lord, to whom shall we go?" And then he said, "THOU HAST THE *WORDS* OF ETERNAL LIFE."

In I Peter 1:18—25 we read, "Forasmuch as ye know that ye were not redeemed with corruptible things, as silver and gold, from your vain conversation received by tradition from your fathers; but with the precious blood of Christ, as of a lamb without blemish and without spot: Who verily was foreordained before the foundation of the world, but was manifest in these last times for you. Who by Him do believe in God, that raised Him up from the dead, and gave Him glory; that your faith and hope might be in God. Seeing ye have *purified your souls* in obeying the truth through the Spirit unto unfeigned love of the brethren, see that ye love one another with a pure heart fervently: *Being born again, not of corruptible seed, but of incorruptible, by the WORD OF GOD, which liveth and abideth for ever.* For all flesh is as grass, and all the glory of man as the flower of grass. The grass withereth, and the flower thereof falleth away: *but the WORD OF THE LORD endureth for ever.* And this is the WORD which by the Gospel is preached unto you."

Notice: We are purified in our souls by obeying the *truth*—and the truth is the WORD. We are born again—not through seed that corrupt, but through *incorruptible seed, the WORD of God.* And whereas all flesh is transient—like the grass it is here today, gone tomorrow—*the WORD of the Lord is eternal,* enduring forever. Thus eternal life comes through the WORD of the living God.

"In the beginning was the WORD, and the WORD was

44

with God, and the WORD was God" (John 1:1).

"And the WORD was made flesh, and dwelt among us, (and we beheld His glory, the glory as of the only begotten of the Father,) full of grace and truth" (John 1:14).

"No man hath seen God at any time; the only begotten Son, which is in the bosom of the Father, He hath declared Him" (John 1:18).

"Verily, verily, I say unto you, He that heareth my WORD, and believeth on Him that sent me, hath everlasting life, and shall not come into condemnation; but is passed from death unto life" (John 5:24).

The First Convert Among the Gentiles

We find this account in the tenth chapter of Acts, where Peter carried the message of saving grace to the house of Cornelius. The Scripture tells us, "There was a certain man in Caesarea called Cornelius, a centurion of the band called the Italian band, a devout man, and one that feared God with all his house, which gave much alms to the people, and prayed to God alway. He saw in a vision evidently about the ninth hour of the day an angel of God coming in to him, and saying unto him, Cornelius. And when he looked on him, he was afraid, and said, What is it, Lord? And he said unto him, Thy prayers and thine alms are come up for a memorial before God. And now send men to Joppa, and call for one Simon, whose surname is Peter: He lodgeth with one Simon a tanner, whose house is by the sea side: he shall tell thee what thou oughtest to do" (Acts 10:1–6).

In Acts 11:13,14 we read, "And he (Cornelius) shewed us how he had seen an angel in his house, which stood and said unto him, Send men to Joppa, and call for Simon, whose surname is Peter; *who shall tell thee WORDS,*

45

whereby thou and all thy house shall be saved."

Notice that the angel told Cornelius that Peter would give him WORDS—not rituals, dogmas, doctrines or traditions of men, but WORDS; and Acts 10:34–43 records the sermon Peter preached that day. In verse 34 we read, *"Then Peter opened his mouth"*—not his briefcase, not his sermon notes—*"and said, Of a truth I perceive that God is no respecter of persons."* Here Peter is preaching John 3:16 and John 6:37. *"Whosoever"*—ALL are included— Jew, Gentile, rich, poor, bond, free. Regardless of race, creed, or color, God is no respecter of persons.

"And we are witnesses of all things which He did both in the land of the Jews, and in Jerusalem; whom they slew and hanged on a tree" (Acts 10:39). Here Peter points to the crucifixion of Jesus. He preached the cross, the shed blood, the sacrificial death of the Lamb without spot or blemish.

"Him God raised up the third day, and shewed Him openly" (v. 40). Here he preached the resurrection. There were those who *denied* the resurrection, and today some still deny that Christ rose bodily; but Paul said to the Corinthians, "If there be no resurrection of the dead, then is Christ not risen: and *if Christ be not risen, then is our preaching vain, and your faith is also vain.* Yea, and we are found false witnesses of God; because we have testified of God that He raised up Christ: whom He raised not up, if so be that the dead rise not. For if the dead rise not, then is not Christ raised: and *if Christ be not raised, your faith is vain; ye are yet in your sins.* Then they also which are fallen asleep in Christ are perished. If in this life only we have hope in Christ, we are of all men most miserable" (I Cor. 15:13–19).

"To Him give all the prophets witness, that through

His name whosoever believeth in Him shall receive remission of sins" (v. 43).   Again Peter points out that regardless of who a person is, if that person believes on Jesus, God forgives his sins. "Whosoever"—any and ALL—can come to God through Christ.

Now notice verse 44: *"While Peter yet spakę these WORDS, the Holy Ghost fell on all them which heard the WORD!"*

"Faith cometh by hearing, and hearing by the Word of God" (Rom. 10:17).   Faith brings saving grace, and by grace we are saved. Cornelius and the people in his house heard the Word, they believed the Word, they received the gift of the Holy Spirit, they spoke with tongues and magnified God.

WORDS brought salvation to the house of Cornelius— and WORDS will bring salvation to *your* house and to your heart (John 5:24; 12:48).

The First Convert In Europe

"And a certain woman named Lydia, a seller of purple, of the city of Thyatira, which worshipped God, heard us: whose heart the Lord opened, that she attended unto the things which were spoken of Paul. And when she was baptized, and her household, she besought us, saying, If ye have judged me to be faithful to the Lord, come into my house, and abide there . . ." (Acts 16:14,15).

Acts 16 is a tremendous chapter on salvation; it gives an account of three outstanding conversions, the first of which we have just quoted. Lydia was a merchant, "a seller of purple," and since only kings and rich men could afford purple and fine linen in those days, we know that Lydia was among the elite. But she was also the teacher of a ladies' Bible class which met "by a river side." Paul was invited to speak at one of these meetings, and you may rest assured that whenever and wherever Paul taught, his teaching concerned the cross and the atoning blood of the Lamb of God. As he spoke to these ladies, the Lord opened Lydia's heart and "she attended unto the things which were spoken of Paul."

I repeat — the Word brings faith, faith brings saving grace, and thus the engrafted Word saves the soul. Lydia *listened* to the Word, she *received* the Word, she was saved — and she invited Paul and Silas to make her home their headquarters in that city.

The Fortuneteller Saved

"And it came to pass, as we went to prayer, a certain damsel possessed with a spirit of divination met us, which brought her masters much gain by soothsaying: The same followed Paul and us, and cried, saying, These men are the servants of the most high God, which shew unto us the way of salvation. And this did she many days. But Paul, being grieved, turned and said to the spirit, I command thee in the name of Jesus Christ to come out of her. And he came out the same hour.

"And when her masters saw that the hope of their gains was gone, they caught Paul and Silas, and drew them into the marketplace unto the rulers, and brought them to the magistrates, saying, These men, being Jews, do exceedingly trouble our city, and teach customs, which are not lawful for us to receive, neither to observe, being Romans. And the multitude rose up together against them: and the magistrates rent off their clothes, and commanded to beat them. And when they had laid many stripes upon them, they cast them into prison, charging the jailor to keep them safely: Who, having received such a charge, thrust them into the inner prison, and made their feet fast in the stocks" (Acts 16:16—24).

The only way for any person to know the way of salvation is to hear the Word of God. This girl followed Paul and Silas many days, saying that they were servants of "the most high God," and that they were showing the way of salvation. This proved that she *listened* to their teaching; by the power of the name of Jesus the evil spirit was cast out, she *believed* the Word, and she was saved. She gave up her fortunetelling, making her masters very angry— so angry that they had Paul and Silas arrested, brought into the marketplace before the rulers, and soundly beaten. They then had them thrown into prison, into the inner cell, and even "made their feet fast in the stocks." I do not doubt that Paul and Silas went to bed without their supper that night—but it was worth it because they had given the bread of life to a poor, demented girl! They had given her the Word of the living God, and in spite of their pitiful situation they sang and praised God in the night.

The Philippian Jailer Saved

"And at midnight Paul and Silas prayed, and sang praises unto God: and the prisoners heard them. And suddenly there was a great earthquake, so that the foundations of the prison were shaken: and immediately all the doors were opened, and every one's bands were loosed. And the keeper of the prison awaking out of his sleep, and seeing the prison doors open, he drew out his sword, and would have killed himself, supposing that the prisoners had been fled. But Paul cried with a loud voice, saying, Do thyself no harm: for we are all here. Then he called for a light, and sprang in, and came trembling, and fell down before Paul and Silas, and brought them out, and said, Sirs, what must I do to be saved? And they said, Believe on the Lord Jesus Christ, and thou shalt be saved, and thy house. *And they spake unto him the WORD of the Lord*, and to all that were in his house. And he took them the same hour of the night, and washed their stripes; and was baptized, he and all his, straightway. And when he had brought them into his house, he set meat before them, and rejoiced, believing in God with all his house" (Acts 16:25—34).

As Paul and Silas sang and prayed at midnight the prisoners heard them — but GOD heard them too; and He answered with an earthquake that shook the very foundations of the prison, opened every door, and loosed every prisoner from his chains. When the jailer awakened and realized that the prison doors were open and the prisoners were free, he drew his sword and would have taken his own life — but Paul called out to him, "Do thyself no harm! *We are all here.*"

This must have surprised the jailer beyond measure. What kind of prisoner would stay in jail when there was opportunity to escape? He called for a light, and springing in where Paul and Silas were he fell down before them, and in fear and trembling asked a question: *"Sirs, what must I do to be saved?"* The answer Paul and Silas gave him was simple and to the point. They said, *"Believe on the Lord Jesus Christ*—and thou shalt be saved, and thy house."

This jailer was an unbeliever, a pagan. It is very likely that he had never heard a message on salvation. He knew nothing of the grace of God nor of the saving power of Jesus. Yet you will notice that he did not ask Paul and Silas what he must do to be "good," or what he must do to become a church member. He wanted to be *saved*—and the way to be saved is to hear the Word of God, for faith comes by hearing and hearing by the Word (Rom. 10:17). So Paul and Silas *"spake unto him the WORD of the Lord,* and to all that were in his house."

Yes, Paul and Silas conducted an old-fashioned Bible class in the jailer's home, and the Scripture tells us that he "washed their stripes" — in other words, he tended the wounds caused by the beating, he fed them, "AND REJOICED, BELIEVING IN GOD WITH ALL HIS HOUSE!"

50

Lydia was saved because she "attended unto the things spoken by Paul"—and Paul spoke the Word of the Lord.

The *fortuneteller* was saved because she *confessed and believed* "the way of salvation" taught by Paul and Silas. She recognized them as servants of "the most high God," and she believed the *Word* of God.

The *jailer* was saved because he heard and believed the Word of the Lord. "Lord, to whom shall we go? THOU hast the WORDS of eternal life."

Are YOU Saved?

Now I did not ask if you are a church member, nor if you have "religion." I did not ask if you are living a "good" life, nor if you are going about doing "good works." I did not ask if you are giving liberally to the church, nor if you have been baptized. I asked, "Are you SAVED?" Do you remember a time—not necessarily a date, a day, or a time of day—but an *experience* with God? Do you recall some time, somewhere, when you heard the Word of God and put your trust in the shed blood of Jesus? Perhaps you were in a church, maybe you read a Gospel tract, it may be you heard a street preacher; but somewhere, in some way, you got hold of the Word of God, you were convicted of your sin and you realized that you needed a Saviour; and then and there you asked the Lord to save you, and you put your trust in Jesus. Do you remember such an experience? If you do not, you had better *have* such an experience—the sooner the better. God grant this be the day, this be the moment, when you realize your lost condition, confess your sins to God, and ask Him to save you for Christ's sake. It is not God's will that you perish; it is His will and His joy to save all who will come to Him by Christ Jesus.

51

"As many as received Him, to them gave He power to become the sons of God, even to them that believe on His name: Which were born, not of blood, nor of the will of the flesh, nor of the will of man, BUT OF GOD" (John 1:12,13).

". . . Behold, *now* is the accepted time; behold, *now* is the day of salvation" (II Cor. 6:2).

Jesus said to the Jews, "Ye *will not* come to me, that ye might have life" (John 5:40). If YOU spend eternity in hell, it will not be by the will of God, but because you WILL NOT come to Jesus that you might have life!

"HOW SHALL WE ESCAPE?"

"HOW SHALL WE ESCAPE?"

"Therefore we ought to give the more earnest heed to the things which we have heard, lest at any time we should let them slip. For if the word spoken by angels was stedfast, and every transgression and disobedience received a just recompence of reward; *how shall we escape, if we neglect so great salvation*; which at the first began to be spoken by the Lord, and was confirmed unto us by them that heard Him; God also bearing them witness, both with signs and wonders, and with divers miracles, and gifts of the Holy Ghost, according to His own will?" (Heb. 2:1–4).

What's *great* about salvation? It is daily preached that all one need do to become the *recipient* of salvation is to believe on the Lord Jesus Christ and His finished work – believe in His virgin birth, His crucifixion, resurrection, and ascension; all a poor sinner can do to become a child of God is to receive Jesus by faith on the terms of what the Bible says about Him. Did someone ask, "If salvation is the gift of God, if it cannot be earned, bought, or merited, *THEN WHAT'S SO GREAT ABOUT IT*?"

For more than a quarter of a century I have preached salvation by grace – not by works of righteousness, but according to God's mercy He saves us. We cannot *pay* for our salvation – it is beyond price (I Pet. 1:18–20). We cannot *earn* salvation, because all of our righteousnesses are as filthy rags in God's sight (Isa. 64:6). We could speak with the tongues of angels, we could possess the gift of prophecy and the faith to move mountains, we could give our earthly possessions to the poor and give our body to be burned at the stake – but in spite of all that, if we have failed to receive Jesus by faith we are hopelessly lost! I

55

have preached that the beggar in rags can be saved just as quickly and as surely as the multimillionaire can be saved—and vice versa. The vilest drunk can be saved in the twinkling of an eye if he will only exercise the faith of a little child and believe in the finished work of Jesus Christ. Salvation is within the reach of all—rich or poor, bond or free, wise or foolish, learned or unlearned—*"whosoever will"* can have salvation simply by coming to God through the shed blood of His Son, Jesus Christ. Yes, salvation is free—but it is also "GREAT":

OUR SALVATION IS GREAT IN ITS COST

"What? Know ye not that your body is the temple of the Holy Ghost which is in you, which ye have of God, and ye are not your own? FOR YE ARE BOUGHT WITH A PRICE: therefore glorify God in your body, and in your spirit, which are God's" (I Cor. 6:19,20).

"YE ARE BOUGHT WITH A PRICE; be not ye the servants of men" (I Cor. 7:23).

If a diamond or a string of pearls costs thousands of dollars we say it is great in its cost—meaning, it is *valuable*. A piece of property which costs tens of thousands of dollars is spoken of as valuable because of its great cost. We are prone to value things according to the dollar-mark, the monetary value placed upon them; and yet *Jesus* asked, *"What is a man profited, if he shall gain the whole world, and lose his own soul? or what shall a man give in exchange for his soul?"* (Matt. 16:26). I repeat the question: What shall a man (one man, ANY man) profit, even though he may gain the whole world, if he loses his own soul? One man—one soul—balanced against all the wealth of all the world!

Let your imagination run wild for a moment: Visualize

56

all the diamonds, rubies, and assorted jewels in the world piled in one giant heap. Then see all of earth's multiplied billions of dollars stacked on top of all the jewels – one gigantic mound of gold, silver, precious stones, all the wealth of all the world. Now against that great mountain of earth's wealth, place one poor, helpless sinner – and consider what Jesus said: If one man could *gain* the whole world and all of its wealth, and yet lose his own soul, he would be profited nothing!

I have said that in order to say this: *If one mortal soul is worth more than all the wealth this world holds, how valuable is the blood of Jesus!* HE purchased salvation for every soul on earth, every soul who ever lived or ever will live – and *ONE sinner* is worth more than all the riches of the universe. Think of the worth of our great salvation, purchased by the Son of God at the cost of His own precious blood.

Paul reminded the Corinthian Christians that they were "bought with a price," and in writing to the Romans he *named* the price God paid that we might become His children:

"For all have sinned, and come short of the glory of God; being justified freely by His grace *through the redemption that is in Christ Jesus: Whom God hath set forth to be a propitiation through faith in His blood, to declare His righteousness for the remission of sins that are past, through the forbearance of God; to declare, I say, at this time His righteousness: that He might be just, and the Justifier of him which believeth in Jesus.* Where is boasting then? It is excluded. By what law? of works? Nay! but by the law of faith. Therefore we conclude that a man is justified by faith without the deeds of the law" (Rom. 3:23–28).

We have redemption in Christ Jesus *through faith in*

57

His BLOOD. Redemption means that God has redeemed (bought back) something that was lost. Adam, in the Garden of Eden, sold out to Satan. Jesus, the last Adam, bought back all that the first Adam surrendered to the devil. Jesus, on the Mount of Temptation, refused to sell out to Satan. God's Word tells us that He was tempted in all points as WE are tempted, yet He was without sin. He faced the lust of the flesh, the lust of the eye, the pride of life – but in every instance He answered Satan with the Word of God, and at last the devil left Him and angels came and ministered to Him. (Study Matthew 4:1–11 for the detailed account.) Christ Jesus came into the world to pay the sin-debt, to redeem; and He DID purchase redemption for the sinner through His precious blood.

To the Ephesians Paul wrote, "Having predestinated us unto the adoption of children by Jesus Christ to Himself, according to the good pleasure of His will, TO THE PRAISE OF THE GLORY OF HIS GRACE, WHEREIN HE HATH MADE US ACCEPTED IN THE BELOVED. IN WHOM WE HAVE REDEMPTION THROUGH HIS BLOOD, THE FORGIVENESS OF SINS, ACCORDING TO THE RICHES OF HIS GRACE" (Eph. 1:5–7).

The price of redemption—a price that had to be paid before WE could become the sons of God—was paid with the precious blood of the Lamb of God.

Under inspiration of the Holy Ghost, Peter explains it thus: *"Forasmuch as ye know that ye were not redeemed with corruptible things, as silver and gold,* from your vain conversation received by tradition from your fathers; but WITH THE PRECIOUS BLOOD OF CHRIST, as of a lamb without blemish and without spot: who verily was foreordained BEFORE THE FOUNDATION OF THE WORLD, but was manifest in these last times for you" (I Pet. 1:18–20).

"*Things*"—silver, gold, pearls, diamonds, rubies, millions in money—cannot redeem us, for things of earth are corruptible. We are redeemed with the *precious* blood of Christ. Peter could have said "powerful" blood, he could have referred to the "sacred" blood or to the "divine" blood; but he used none of those descriptive words. He used the word mothers use when they speak of a new-born babe: he said "*PRECIOUS blood.*" Many paragraphs could be written, many sermons could be preached, about those two words, but let me say just this: The fact that the blood is referred to as *precious* emphasizes the great cost of redemption, the great price paid for this GREAT SALVATION that can be ours if we do not neglect to receive Jesus by faith.

Who PAID this cost of redemption? *God the Father* paid a tremendous price that we might be redeemed: *it cost Him His only begotten Son.* For thirty-three and one-half years Jesus was in "the far country" away from the Father's bosom:

"In the beginning was the Word, and the Word was with God, and the Word was God. The same was in the beginning with God. . . And the Word was made flesh, and dwelt among us, (and we beheld His glory, the glory as of the only begotten of the Father,) full of grace and truth. . . *No man hath seen God at any time; the only begotten Son, which is in the bosom of the Father, He hath declared Him*" (John 1:1, 2, 14, 18).

We know that "the Word" was Jesus. He was in the beginning with the Father, He was in the *bosom* of the Father—and what closer fellowship could Father and Son have? Jesus was precious to the heavenly Father, but He stepped from the bosom of the Father to the womb of the virgin and was born in a body like unto our body, that He might redeem us from the curse of sin and the damnation of hell:

"When the fulness of the time was come, God sent forth His Son, made of a woman, made under the law, to redeem them that were under the law, that we might receive the adoption of sons" (Gal. 4:4,5).

"God is love" (I John 4:8); He loved His only begotten Son and fellowshipped with Him. They had sweet communion together — but God gave Him up and sent Him forth that He might pay the sin-debt and purchase our redemption. Before the foundation of the world was laid, Father, Son, and Holy Ghost agreed that the beloved Son would give His precious blood that we might have salvation (I Pet. 1:18–20; John 3:16,17).

In II Corinthians 5:21 we read, "For He (God) hath made Him (Jesus) to be sin for us, who knew no sin (Jesus was sinless); that we might be made the righteousness of God in Him." Yes, it was GOD who made Jesus "to be sin for us" — but hear these words from the pen of the prophet Isaiah:

"Surely He (Jesus) hath borne our griefs, and carried our sorrows: yet we did esteem Him stricken, SMITTEN OF GOD, and afflicted. But He was wounded for our transgressions, He was bruised for our iniquities: the chastisement of our peace was upon Him; and with His stripes we are healed. All we like sheep have gone astray; we have turned every one to his own way; AND THE LORD HATH LAID ON HIM THE INIQUITY OF US ALL" (Isa. 53:4–6).

God paid the dearest at the cross: "Now from the sixth hour there was darkness over all the land unto the ninth hour. And about the ninth hour Jesus cried with a loud voice, saying, Eli, Eli, lama sabachthani? That is to say, *My God, my God, why hast thou forsaken me?* Some

60

of them that stood there, when they heard that, said, This
man calleth for Elias. And straightway one of them ran,
and took a spunge, and filled it with vinegar, and put it
on a reed, and gave Him to drink. The rest said, Let be,
let us see whether Elias will come to save Him. Jesus,
when He had cried again with a loud voice, yielded up
the ghost'' (Matt. 27:45–50).

Dear reader, God *literally turned His head* while Jesus
paid the sin-debt and purchased redemption by the shedding
of His precious blood, that "so great salvation" might be
ours! ". . . Christ also suffered for us, leaving us an
example, that ye should follow His steps: Who did no sin,
neither was guile found in His mouth: Who, when He was
reviled, reviled not again; when He suffered, He threatened
not; but committed Himself to Him that judgeth righteously:
*Who His own self bare our sins in His own body on the
tree, that WE, being dead to sins, should live unto righteousness: by whose stripes ye were healed*'' (I Pet.
2:21–24).

Because God is God, He cannot look upon sin. Jesus
bore *our* sins in His body on the cross; therefore it was a
divine imperative that God turn His head while Jesus died.
While Jesus paid the sin-debt, God turned away from Him;
and for that bitter, bitter moment when He hung on the
cross, bearing the sins of the world, He lost sight of the
Father's face and cried out, "My God! My God! Why hast
thou forsaken me?"

It was God who purposed the death of Christ (Rom.
3:25). Jesus on the cross was God's love on display, God's
best for earth's worst: "God commendeth His love toward
us, in that, while we were yet sinners, Christ died for us"
(Rom. 5:8). The word "commend" in the original language
means "to place together; of persons, to introduce to one's

61

acquaintance and favorable notice, hence to commend, to represent as worthy."

It was God who provided the possibility of Jesus' dying: "But we see Jesus, who was made a little lower than the angels for the suffering of death, crowned with glory and honour; that He *by the grace of God* should taste death for every man" (Heb. 2:9). "There is therefore now no condemnation to them which are in Christ Jesus, who walk not after the flesh, but after the Spirit. For the law of the Spirit of life in Christ Jesus hath made me free from the law of sin and death. For what the law could not do, in that it was weak through the flesh, *GOD sending His own Son in the likeness of sinful flesh, and for sin, condemned sin in the flesh*: that the righteousness of the law might be fulfilled in us, who walk not after the flesh, but after the Spirit" (Rom. 8:1–4).

God gave His very best—His own Son: "He that spared not His own Son, but delivered Him up for us all, how shall He not with Him also freely give us all things?" (Rom. 8:32). God did not spare the angels from hell and chains of darkness when they rebelled against Him (II Pet. 2:4). He did not spare the ungodly people of Noah's day when they refused to heed His warning (II Pet. 2:5). He did not spare Israel, although that nation was the apple of His eye. When unbelief caused them to turn their backs upon Him He did not spare them from being cut off from blessing (Rom. 11:21); and He did not spare Himself from smiting the Son when He gave Him on the cross to be our substitute.

WHY did God not spare Jesus? What God demanded, only God could provide; therefore if WE were to be spared the damnation of hell, God could not spare His Son. Jesus was God incarnate—the only righteous One, and we are spared for the sake of that One. God's stroke fell on *Him*, the Lamb without spot or blemish:

"He was taken from prison and from judgment: and who shall declare His generation? for He was cut off out of the land of the living: for the transgression of my people was He stricken. And He made His grave with the wicked, and with the rich in His death; because He had done no violence, neither was any deceit in His mouth. YET IT PLEASED THE LORD TO BRUISE HIM; HE HATH PUT HIM TO GRIEF: when thou shalt make His soul an offering for sin, He shall see His seed, He shall prolong His days, and the pleasure of the Lord shall prosper in His hand" (Isa. 53:8–10).

Jesus the Son also paid a tremendous price that we might be redeemed. From John's Gospel we learned that the Word was in the beginning with God, the Word was God, and the Word was made flesh. Jesus left the Father's bosom and became flesh, and in flesh He put grace and truth on display and brought them down to man. Salvation is ours because of God's grace – we are saved by God's grace through faith. It was by God's grace that Jesus was permitted to die for us, and if we are to fully appreciate our great salvation we must understand (as far as is humanly possible) the tremendous price Jesus paid that we might be saved.

In Ephesians 3:8,9 Paul gives a Bible definition of grace. He said, "Unto me, who am less than the least of all saints, is this grace given, that I should preach among the Gentiles *the unsearchable riches of Christ; and to make all men see what is the fellowship of the mystery, which from the beginning of the world hath been hid in God,* who created all things by Jesus Christ."

In II Corinthians 8:9 we read, "For ye know the grace

63

of our Lord Jesus Christ, that, though He was rich, yet for your sakes He became poor, that ye through His poverty might be rich."

If we are ever to understand the grace of our Lord Jesus Christ, it is necessary that we understand His riches—what He possessed before He left the Father's house and came to earth's poverty that WE might become rich in Him through God's marvelous grace. We cannot begin to know the meaning of *grace* until we realize, to some degree at least, the riches of Christ—riches which include all that He was in the beginning and all that He possessed in the eternal ages behind us. In some small measure, we must understand the depth of His poverty and humiliation. If we are to understand grace, we must enter into the meaning of the sufferings of the Lamb of God—He who sacrificed heaven's glory and came to earth to a people who branded Him the lowest of humanity!

Then, to know, appreciate, and understand grace, we must understand the riches WE possess when we possess Christ, and the exceeding heights to which we are lifted when HE lifts us from the miry clay to the solid rock. We must understand the blessings God has purposed (and does bestow upon us) in Christ and for Christ's sake.

I realize that we cannot fully *define* grace, nor will we ever fully *understand* God's marvelous grace; but that is no excuse for our failing to study and understand all that we *can* understand about the riches of our Saviour and the poverty He suffered that we might be made rich in Him.

Paul speaks of "*the UNSEARCHABLE riches of Christ*" (Eph. 3:8); and in Ephesians 1:18 he speaks of "the riches of the glory of (Christ's) inheritance in the saints." The Apostle Paul possessed unusual knowledge

64

of the riches of Christ—a knowledge given to him by revelation, not attained through his own ability. God revealed many things to this minister to the Gentiles, things never before revealed to any of the prophets. *Our* purpose is to seek knowledge from the Word of God concerning the riches of Christ in the ages behind us, the riches He left when He left the bosom of the Father to come to earth in a body of flesh:

1. *Christ was rich in possessions:*

"For by Him were all things created, that are in heaven, and that are in earth, visible and invisible, whether they be thrones, or dominions, or principalities, or powers: all things were created BY Him, and FOR Him" (Col. 1:16).

The heavens, all the planets, declare and show forth the glory of our Lord (Psalm 19:1). The sun, the moon, the billions of štars—all are the work of His fingers, created by Him in the eternity behind us. No wonder the Psalmist cried out, "PRAISE YE THE LORD! Praise ye the Lord from the heavens: praise Him in the heights. Praise ye Him, all His angels: praise ye Him, all His hosts. Praise ye Him, sun and moon: praise Him, all ye stars of light. Praise Him, ye heavens of heavens, and ye waters that be above the heavens. Let them praise the name of the Lord: for He commanded, and they were created. He hath also stablished them for ever and ever: He hath made a decree which shall not pass" (Psalm 148:1–6).

2. *Christ was rich in glory:*

In John 17:5 Jesus prayed, "O Father, glorify thou me with thine own self *with the glory which I had with thee before the world was.*" Nowhere in His Word does God spell out the glory Christ had with Him before the world was — and if that glory *were* defined or outlined we

65

could not understand or appreciate it. Words that can be uttered by man could never touch the hem of the garment in describing the glory Jesus had with the Father in the beginning before the world was; and even if man's language could describe and express that glory, finite minds could not grasp it. God found it sufficient to say that "all things" were created by Him and for Him—and when the Bible says "all things" it means exactly that—ALL things. Yes, Christ was rich in glory before ever the world was created.

3. *Christ was rich in that He was one with God:*

Paul tells us in Philippians 2:6 that Christ, "being in the form of God, thought it not robbery to be *equal with God.*" Christ Jesus was God. He was God before He became Jesus in flesh. *Christ* is His name in Deity; *Jesus* is His name as Saviour. Joseph and Mary were instructed to name Him JESUS because He would save His people from their sins. In the beginning, Christ was with God, Christ *was* God (John 1:1), and in Him dwelt all the fulness of the Godhead (Col. 2:9).

4. *Christ was rich in His person:*

According to Hebrews 1:3, Christ was *the brightness of God's glory, "the express image* (exact expression) *of His person."* The same holy, divine attributes that enriched the person of Almighty God also enriched the person of Christ Jesus, God's only begotten Son.

5. *Christ was rich in power:*

David, a man after God's own heart, declared, "I will sing of thy power" (Psalm 59:16). God is the *source* of all power—and have you ever considered that all things created by Him are *stored* with power? In these days of unusual learning and wisdom in the fields of science and physics, we can appreciate more than ever before the power contained in the things around us. When we consider that all things created by Christ are stored with power, when we consider the atomic bomb, atomic power, the hydrogen bomb, and other discoveries of our day, then we can begin to appreciate, in some small measure, the exceeding riches of His power. If by simply *speaking words* Christ made the worlds, what *could* He do if He should demonstrate ALL of His great power in a *moment*? He will do that, one of these glorious days. At His speaking of a word, this earth will melt; and by His speaking a word, a new heaven and a new earth will come into being. All things will be created new — and this will happen through HIS POWER.

6. *Christ was rich in worship:*

The second Person of the Trinity was worshipped as no other heavenly being has ever been worshipped. We catch a glimpse of this when the earth was created, "when the morning stars sang together, and all the sons of God shouted for joy" (Job 38:7). The angels of God worshipped the Son and praised His name. It is true that angels are ministering spirits to the heirs of salvation (Heb. 1:14); but they also serve God, do His will, and worship the Son, "for the Lord is a great God, and a great King above *all* gods. . . O come, let us worship and bow down: let us kneel before the Lord our Maker" (Psalm 95:3,6). In Psalm 29:2 we read, "Give unto the Lord the glory due unto His name; worship the Lord in the beauty of holiness." Yes, Christ Jesus was exceedingly rich in worship.

7. *Christ was rich in His Father's love:*

In the beginning, Christ the Son and Jehovah God the Father were ONE (John 1:1). There was never one shadow of separation between God the Father, Christ the Son, and the Holy Spirit—the three Persons who make up the Triune Godhead.

In John 3:31—35 we read, "*He that cometh from above is above ALL*: he that is of the earth is earthly, and speaketh of the earth: *HE THAT COMETH FROM HEAVEN IS ABOVE ALL.* And what He hath seen and heard, that He testifieth; and no man receiveth His testimony. He that hath received His testimony hath set to his seal that God is true. *FOR HE WHOM GOD HATH SENT SPEAKETH THE WORDS OF GOD: FOR GOD GIVETH NOT THE SPIRIT BY MEASURE UNTO HIM. THE FATHER LOVETH THE SON, AND HATH GIVEN ALL THINGS INTO HIS HAND.*"

God the Father spoke of Christ as His "*only begotten*" Son; and during His earthly ministry He audibly announced Him as "*my beloved Son*, in whom I am well pleased" (Matt. 3:17; 17:5).

Yes, our Lord was "unsearchably" rich—in possessions, in glory, in His relationship to God. He was rich in His person as Jesus Christ the only begotten Son, He was rich in power, in worship, and in His Father's love; but in II Corinthians 8:9 we read:

"For ye know the grace of our Lord Jesus Christ, that, *though He was rich, yet for your sakes He became poor, that ye through His poverty might be rich.*"

1. Christ became poor in possessions:

When Jesus was born, neither Joseph nor Mary had enough money or influence to obtain a room with a bed and the baby Jesus was born in a stable, a sheep barn. Born into the humble home of a carpenter, He without a doubt followed Joseph's trade as a lad and as a young man.

When He began His public ministry, He was a preacher without a place to call home. He said, "The foxes have holes, and the birds of the air have nests; *but the Son of man hath not where to lay His head*" (Matt. 8:20). When the disciples of John asked, "Master, where dwellest thou?" He said to them, "Come and see" (John 1:35–39). But the Scripture is silent as to what those two disciples saw or experienced that day, from the standpoint of physical comforts, when they went home with Jesus.

When the question about taxes came up, Jesus had no money with which to pay His taxes, and He said to Peter, ". . . Go thou to the sea, and cast an hook, and take up the fish that first cometh up; and when thou hast opened his mouth, thou shalt find a piece of money: that take, and give unto them for me and thee" (Matt. 17:24–27). On another occasion, when the multitudes pressed too heavily about Him, He borrowed a boat to use as a pulpit from which to preach to the crowd on the shore (Matt. 13:2). He borrowed a little boy's lunch of five loaves and two small fishes and fed five thousand guests who had come to hear Him preach (John 6:1–14). He was so poor in earthly possessions that when He died He was buried in a borrowed tomb.

But the poverty of Christ Jesus the Son of God included far more than lack of a place to lay His head, far more than being poverty-stricken concerning earthly comforts. As we study this subject in the Word of God we see a tremendous contrast between *the RICHES of Christ Jesus* with the Father, and *the POVERTY of Jesus, Saviour*, as He tabernacled among men.

2. *Jesus was poor in glory:*

When He came to earth to pay the sin-debt, He laid

aside the glory He had had with the Father, and lived as an unknown, unrecognized person. For thirty years He moved among men—and they knew Him not! Even when He came on the scene of His public ministry, *His own* refused to receive Him (John 1:11). According to His own testimony, most of those who followed Him did so because of the loaves and fishes, and because He was able to heal their diseases and restore the dead to life. The masses followed Him for awhile, it is true; but they followed Him for what they could get from Him and for what He could do for them, and not because He was the Son of God. Among men, Jesus was indeed poor in glory. Men spat upon Him, they ridiculed Him, on occasion they would have *stoned* Him. They would have thrown Him over a precipice had it not been foreordained of God that He should pay the sin-debt on the cross.

3. *Jesus was poor in praise:*

Instead of being praised, He was blasphemed. Instead of being hailed as the Son of God, He was accused of being an illegitimate. His own people, the Jews, said to Him, "*Abraham* is *our* father. . . *We* be not born of fornication" (John 8:39—41 in part), thus suggesting that Jesus was a child of fornication. He was set at nought, mistreated, and finally *betrayed* into the hands of His enemies to be crucified. Even as He hung on the cross they jeered, taunted, and mocked Him as He died! Certainly He was poor in praise on earth.

4. *Jesus was poor in physical rest:*

He was often weary in body. Luke 8:22—25 tells of His falling asleep in a ship while He and His disciples were crossing a lake, and when a storm arose and the ship was near to being capsized by the waves, the disciples had to waken Him. "Then He arose, and rebuked the wind and the raging of the water: and they ceased, and there was a calm."

On another occasion He stopped at Jacob's well to rest, "being *wearied* with His journey"—and no doubt hungry, too, because the Scripture tells us that His disciples "were gone away unto the city to buy meat." Yet even as He rested there, He gave the water of life to the poor, sinful Samaritan woman, she was saved, and her glorious testimony led to a revival among the Samaritans. You can read the full and detailed account in the fourth chapter of John's Gospel.

Isaiah 50:6 tells us that He gave His back to the smiters and His cheeks to them that plucked off the hair. We know that He gave His head to those who pressed down the thorns, and His hands and feet to those who drove the spikes. He suffered agony such as no mortal has ever known, or ever *could* know. Yes, Jesus was poor in physical rest—and yet He tenderly invites, "Come unto me, all ye that labour and are heavy laden, *and I will give you REST*" (Matt. 11:28).

5. *Jesus was poor in His person:*

He was the "express image" of God the Father, He was the manifestation of God, full of grace and truth; and yet men did not know Him. He came unto His own, and His own received Him not. To the unbelieving world He was a fraud, an imposter, an illegitimate, a rabble-rouser, a preacher of false doctrine, a disturber of the peace. His enemies could not convict Him of sin, they could not point a finger at His life (John 8:46). Pilate three times declared, "I find no fault in this man." But the glory of His person was veiled. He was very God—yet by men He was reckoned with demons. They said He performed His miracles through the power of Beelzebub, *prince* of demons. He possessed all power, but He never demonstrated that power against His enemies. Finally they arrested Him, nailed Him to a cross, and He died in shame between two thieves! He was indeed poor in His person while He walked this earth.

6.   Jesus was poor in His separation from the Father:

This was true only as He hung on the cross. Throughout the Son's earthly sojourn, God the Father had been His constant companion and guide. Jesus said, "I and my Father are *one* . . . I am in the Father, and the Father in me." Together Jesus and the heavenly Father walked the weary road of His earthly ministry—from His baptism to the cross, from the mount of temptation until in the Garden of Gethsemane He said, "I AM." There they arrested Him and led Him away to be crucified.

But as He hung on the cross, made to be sin for us (II Cor. 5:21), it was a divine imperative that God hide His face from Him. Jesus was bearing the sins of the world—OUR sins—in His own body on the cross, and God the Father cannot look on sin. Therefore as the only begotten Son paid the sin-debt, God turned His head and Jesus cried out, "My God! My God! Why hast thou forsaken me?"

Yes, He who was "unsearchably rich" became poor, that we through His poverty might be made rich in His marvelous, saving grace.

The Pathway of His Humiliation

"Let this mind be in you, which was also in Christ Jesus: Who, being in the form of God, thought it not robbery to be equal with God: but made Himself of no reputation, and took upon Him the form of a servant, and was

72

made in the likeness of men: And being found in fashion as a man, He humbled Himself, and became obedient unto death, even the death of the cross'' (Phil. 2:5–8).

Before His incarnation Christ Jesus had been one with God the Father from all eternity, co-equal with the Father in all things. He was not only *with* God; *He WAS God* — and frequently during His earthly life He spoke of having come forth from heaven, from the heavenly Father:

''For the bread of God is He which cometh down from heaven, and giveth life unto the world'' (John 6:33).

''For I came down from heaven, not to do mine own will, but the will of Him that sent me'' (John 6:38).

''I am that bread of life. Your fathers did eat manna in the wilderness, and are dead. This is the bread which cometh down from heaven, that a man may eat thereof, and not die. I am the living bread which came down from heaven: if any man eat of this bread, he shall live for ever: and the bread that I will give is my flesh, which I will give for the life of the world'' (John 6:48–51).

''Then cried Jesus in the temple as He taught, saying, Ye both know me, and ye know whence I am: and I am not come of myself, but He that sent me is true, whom ye know not. But I know Him: for I am from Him, and He hath sent me'' (John 7:28,29).

''Jesus answered and said unto them, Though I bear record of myself, yet my record is true: for I know whence I came, and whither I go; but ye cannot tell whence I come, and whither I go'' (John 8:14).

''And yet if I judge, my judgment is true: for I am not alone, but I and the Father that sent me'' (John 8:16).

''I am one that bear witness of myself, and the Father

73

that sent me beareth witness of me" (John 8:18).

"I have many things to say and to judge of you: but He that sent me is true; and I speak to the world those things which I have heard of Him" (John 8:26).

"Jesus said unto them, If God were your Father, ye would love me: for I proceeded forth and came from God; neither came I of myself, but He sent me" (John 8:42).

Jesus made it very clear that He came to this earth from God the Father. He came into a world that was wrecked by sin. Men refused to receive Him. "He was in the world, and the world was made by Him, and the world knew Him not. He came unto His own, and His own received Him not" (John 1:10,11). Men hid their faces from the Lord of glory. They said, "We will not have this Man!" From the cradle to the cross—and even to the grave—He was rejected. He was unrecognized by the world at His birth, He was unhonored by the world in His life. He was a stranger to His brethren, an alien to His mother's children (Psalm 69:8). He was hated without a cause. The masses despised Him.

Jesus walked a path of humiliation such as no mortal ever walked. He took upon Himself the form of man—a body of flesh—in order that He might accomplish what the law did not and could not accomplish because of the *weakness* of the flesh (Rom. 8:1–3). His earthly body was subject to hunger, thirst, weariness, even disappointment, just as WE are subject to those physical weaknesses. "Forasmuch then as the children are partakers of flesh and blood, He also Himself likewise took part of the same; that through death He might destroy him that had the power of death, that is, the devil; and deliver them who through fear of death were all their lifetime subject to bondage" (Heb. 2:14,15).

Jesus partook of *man's flesh*, but He received His blood from Almighty God: "Take heed therefore unto yourselves, and to all the flock, over the which the Holy Ghost hath made you overseers, to feed the Church of God, *which He hath purchased WITH HIS OWN BLOOD*" (Acts 20:28).

"Wherefore in all things it behoved Him to be made like unto His brethren, that He might be a merciful and faithful high priest in things pertaining to God, to make reconciliation for the sins of the people" (Heb. 2:17). Jesus is the one Mediator between God and man (I Tim. 2:5).

He took upon Himself the form of a servant. All things were created by Him and for Him — and yet He came to earth not to be ministered unto, but to minister, and to give His life a ransom for the sins of the world. To His disciples He said, "I am among you as he that serveth" (Luke 22:27). In that day it was the duty of a servant to wash the feet of visitors to a home, and John 13:4—16 tells us that Jesus, after the last supper with His disciples, girded Himself with a towel, poured water in a basin, and washed their feet. He came to serve—*and more*: He came to lay His life down that we might have life and have it abundantly.

The final step in the pathway of His humiliation was His obedience unto death—"*even the death of the cross*." On the cross Christ stooped to the lowest depth of His humiliation: He could have died no lower death than on a cross, hanging between two thieves. He was numbered among the transgressors; He was crucified as an imposter, a blasphemer, a political rebel against Rome. It pleased the Lord to bruise Him (Isa. 53:10), and He willingly bore our disgrace and humiliation that we, through faith in His finished work, might be saved!

It cost Jesus the Saviour a tremendous price to purchase our salvation, but thank God *He paid that price in full* when on the cross He cried, "It is finished!" and gave up the ghost.

OUR SALVATION IS GREAT IN ITS SCOPE

There is a teaching abroad in the land that some are elected to be saved while others are elected to be damned. There are those who teach and preach that not all can be saved and that Jesus did not die for all sinners of all ages. Suppose we let the Bible define the scope of the salvation God made possible by setting forth His Son to be the prcpitiation for our sins:

"For God so loved THE WORLD, that He gave His only begotten Son, that WHOSOEVER believeth in Him should not perish, but have everlasting life" (John 3:16). This verse is often referred to as "the Gospel in a nutshell," and there is enough Gospel in it to save the whole world if the world would only hear and believe it! God so loved the *world*—not a certain group, not a certain nationality, not just a select, elect few—but "WHOSOEVER"; and that includes everyone and excludes no one.

"For God sent not His Son into the world to condemn the world; but that the WORLD through Him might be SAVED" (John 3:17). Jesus died for the sins of the *world*, and *whosoever* shall call upon His name shall be saved. *Whosoever is thirsty* may drink of the water of life. He came to save "whosoever will."

I John 2:1,2 tells us, "My little children, these things write I unto you, that ye sin not. And if any man sin, we have an Advocate with the Father, Jesus Christ the righteous: and *He is the propitiation for our sins: and not for our's only, but also for the sins of the WHOLE WORLD.*"

76

Jesus came to the Jew first (Rom. 1:16); He offered salvation first to His own people. When He called the twelve and sent them forth, He instructed them, "Go not into the way of the Gentiles, and into any city of the Samaritans enter ye not: *but go rather to the lost sheep of the house of Israel*" (Matt. 10:5,6). When the Syrophenician woman besought Him to heal her daughter, He replied, "I am not sent but unto the lost sheep of the house of Israel" (Matt. 15:24). Salvation was offered first to the Jews, and Jesus declared to them that the reason they were not saved was because they WOULD NOT COME TO HIM that they might have life (John 5:40). He did not say, "because you are not *elected*," or "because you are not *chosen*," but because you *will not come to me!*"

Grieving over Jerusalem He said, "O Jerusalem, Jerusalem, which killest the prophets, and stonest them that are sent unto thee; how often would I have gathered thy children together, as a hen doth gather her brood under her wings, *and ye would not*! Behold, your house is left unto you desolate: and verily I say unto you, Ye shall not see me, until the time come when ye shall say, Blessed is He that cometh in the name of the Lord" (Luke 13:34,35).

Jesus said, "Come unto me, *all ye that labour and are heavy laden*, and I will give you rest" (Matt. 11:28).

He said, ". . . *Him that cometh to me* I will in no wise cast out" (John 6:37).

In Revelation 22:17 we read, "The Spirit and the bride say, Come. And let him that heareth say, Come. And let him that is athirst come. And WHOSOEVER WILL, let him take the water of life freely."

The Word of God is clear concerning the teaching of election, and it does not teach that some are elected to

77

be saved while others are elected to be damned. II Peter 3:9 plainly tells us that God is "not willing that ANY should perish, *but that ALL should come to repentance.*"

The Bible plainly says that God so loved the WORLD that He gave His only begotten Son that WHOSOEVER—anyone, everyone—who will come to Jesus can be saved; and as for me and my house, we will believe the Word of God. My own heart says with Paul, "Let God be true, but every man a liar" (Rom. 3:4); and if YOU are not saved, it is simply because *you will not come to Jesus*!

Do you know of anything else on earth that *includes everyone* and excludes *no one*? What organization do you know of—political, racial, or religious—that includes everyone and excludes no one? There is nothing else known to man that has the scope of this great salvation — all can participate, all can share in the blessing, all can have a part. No wonder the Apostle Paul asked the searching question, "How shall we escape if we neglect so great salvation?"

OUR SALVATION IS GREAT IN ITS PRESENT PROVISION AND IN ITS CLIMAX

Our great salvation not only provides redemption from the *penalty* of sin, it also provides deliverance from the *power* of sin; and in the by-and-by it will provide deliverance from the very *presence* of sin.

The split second we believe on Jesus we become a child of God, we are born into God's family—and if we live for Jesus through fifty years we are no more *fully* born again than when we first believed. When God "borns" us into the family of heaven, that birth is complete. "Beloved, NOW are we the sons of God . . ." (I John 3:2).

Although we become sons of God the instant we are

78

born again, we are "babes in Christ" and we need to be fed and led. Salvation provides the necessary food and leadership:

"As *newborn babes*, desire the sincere milk of the Word, that ye may grow thereby" (I Pet. 2:2).

"Ye are not in the flesh, but in the Spirit, if so be that the Spirit of God dwell in you. Now if any man have not the Spirit of Christ, he is none of His. . . For as many as are led by the Spirit of God, they are the sons of God. . . . The Spirit (Himself) beareth witness with our spirit, that we are the children of God" (Rom. 8:9, 14, 16).

Our great salvation provides victory over the world, the flesh, and the devil: "There hath no temptation taken you but such as is common to man: but God is faithful, who will not suffer you to be tempted above that ye are able; but will with the temptation also make a way to escape, that ye may be able to bear it" (I Cor. 10:13).

Not only did the Christ leave the Father's bosom and take a body of flesh that He might taste death for every man; not only did He die on the cross that we might have life and have it abundantly; He has also promised never to leave us nor forsake us: ". . . For He hath said, I will never leave thee, nor forsake thee. So that we may boldly say, The Lord is my helper, and I will not fear what man shall do unto me" (Heb. 13:5,6).

Yes, our great salvation provides redemption from the penalty of sin, redemption from the power of sin and temptation, and when Jesus comes for His own we will be delivered from the *presence* of sin:

"I would not have you to be ignorant, brethren, concerning them which are asleep, that ye sorrow not, even as others which have no hope. For if we believe that

79

Jesus died and rose again, even so them also which sleep in Jesus will God bring with Him. For this we say unto you by the Word of the Lord, that we which are alive and remain unto the coming of the Lord shall not prevent them which are asleep. For the Lord Himself shall descend from heaven with a shout, with the voice of the archangel, and with the trump of God: and the dead in Christ shall rise first: Then we which are alive and remain shall be caught up together with them in the clouds, to meet the Lord in the air: and so shall we ever be with the Lord. Wherefore comfort one another with these words'' (I Thess. 4:13–18).

We do not know the day or the hour when Jesus will come, but we do know that one day He WILL descend from heaven—with a shout, with the voice of the archangel, with the trump of God; and at that time the bodies of those who sleep in Christ will be raised incorruptible, the *living* saints will be changed, and together we will be caught up to meet the Lord in the air. This is the promise of God's Word – and God cannot lie.

Jesus said to His disciples, "Let not your heart be troubled: ye believe in God, believe also in me. In my Father's house are many mansions: if it were not so, I would have told you. *I go to prepare a place for YOU.* And if I go and prepare a place for you, *I will come again, and receive you unto myself*; that where I am, there ye may be also'' (John 14:1–3).

Yes, Jesus has gone to prepare a place for us, and that place is described in the twenty-first chapter of Revelation. Read it—and rejoice that one day every born again believer will live in that place—the home Jesus is now preparing for those who put their trust in His finished work and shed blood.

Not only will He take us to live in that glorious place

He is preparing for us, but *He will give us a body capable of enjoying that celestial city*:

"Behold, what manner of love the Father hath bestowed upon us, that we should be called the sons of God: therefore the world knoweth us not, because it knew Him not. *Beloved, NOW are we the sons of God, and it doth not yet appear what we SHALL be: but we know that, when He shall appear, WE SHALL BE LIKE HIM*; *for we shall see Him as He is*" (I John 3:1,2).

We learn from the Word of God that this great salvation is all-sufficient — we are complete in Jesus; for time and for eternity our every need is met in Him. But first we must hear the Gospel, believe on the Lord Jesus Christ, and trust Him as our personal Saviour. He then supplies our *physical* needs, our *spiritual* needs, and our *eternal* needs. His promise is, "Lo, I am with you alway, even to the end" — *and after that*, praise God, He will receive us unto Himself, confess us to the heavenly Father, and we will hear the Father say, "Enter thou into the joys of thy Lord, prepared from the foundation of the world."

"*How SHALL we escape if we neglect so great salvation*?" It is true that the only way to be saved is by God's grace through faith in the Lord Jesus Christ. Jesus is the author and finisher of saving faith, He is the author of salvation, He is the Door to heaven. He is the only Saviour of sinners, the only Mediator between God and man. But beloved, think what it cost God the Father, God the Son, and God the Holy Ghost to make this great salvation possible! It has been paid for in full, it is provided for "whosoever will," and it is all-sufficient: "For in (Christ) dwelleth all the fulness of the Godhead bodily. And YE ARE COMPLETE IN HIM, which is the head of all principality and power" (Col. 2:9,10).

If you are not a believer, receive the Lord Jesus Christ, and God will "born" you into the family of heaven. If you have trusted Jesus as a result of this message, write me and allow me to share the joy of your salvation. Your joy is my reward for preparing this message.

"For by grace are ye saved through faith; and that not of yourselves: it is the gift of God: not of works, lest any man should boast" (Eph. 2:8,9).

'WHAT ACCUSATION BRING YE
AGAINST THIS MAN?''

"WHAT ACCUSATION BRING YE AGAINST THIS MAN?"

"Then led they Jesus from Caiaphas unto the hall of judgment: and it was early; and they themselves went not into the judgment hall, lest they should be defiled; but that they might eat the passover.

"Pilate then went out unto them, and said, What accusation bring ye against this man? They answered and said unto him, If He were not a malefactor, we would not have delivered Him up unto thee. Then said Pilate unto them, Take ye Him, and judge Him according to your law. The Jews therefore said unto him, It is not lawful for us to put any man to death: That the saying of Jesus might be fulfilled, which He spake, signifying what death He should die.

"Then Pilate entered into the judgment hall again, and called Jesus, and said unto Him, Art thou the King of the Jews? Jesus answered him, Sayest thou this thing of thyself, or did others tell it thee of me? Pilate answered, Am I a Jew? Thine own nation and the chief priests have delivered thee unto me: what hast thou done?

"Jesus answered, My kingdom is not of this world: if my kingdom were of this world, then would my servants fight, that I should not be delivered to the Jews: but now is my kingdom not from hence. Pilate therefore said unto Him, Art thou a king then? Jesus answered, Thou sayest that I am a king. To this end was I born, and for this cause came I into the world, that I should bear witness unto the truth. Every one that is of the truth heareth my voice.

"Pilate saith unto Him, What *is* truth? And when he had said this, he went out again unto the Jews, and saith unto them, I find in Him no fault at all. But ye have a custom, that I should release unto you one at the passover: will ye therefore that I release unto you the King of the

Jews? Then cried they all again, saying, Not this man, but Barabbas. Now Barabbas was a robber.

"Then Pilate therefore took Jesus, and scourged Him. And the soldiers platted a crown of thorns, and put it on His head, and they put on Him a purple robe, and said, Hail, King of the Jews! and they smote Him with their hands.

"Pilate therefore went forth again, and saith unto them, Behold, I bring Him forth to you, that ye may know that I find no fault in Him. Then came Jesus forth, wearing the crown of thorns, and the purple robe. And Pilate saith unto them, Behold the man! When the chief priests therefore and officers saw Him, they cried out, saying, Crucify Him, crucify Him. Pilate saith unto them, Take ye Him, and crucify Him: for I find no fault in Him.

"The Jews answered him, We have a law, and by our law He ought to die, because He made Himself the Son of God. When Pilate therefore heard that saying, he was the more afraid; and went again into the judgment hall, and saith unto Jesus, Whence art thou? But Jesus gave him no answer. Then saith Pilate unto Him, Speakest thou not unto me? Knowest thou not that I have power to crucify thee, and have power to release thee?

"Jesus answered, Thou couldest have no power at all against me, except it were given thee from above: therefore he that delivered me unto thee hath the greater sin. And from thenceforth Pilate sought to release Him: but the Jews cried out, saying, If thou let this man go, thou art not Caesar's friend: whosoever maketh himself a king speaketh against Caesar.

"When Pilate therefore heard that saying, he brought Jesus forth, and sat down in the judgment seat in a place that is called the Pavement, but in the Hebrew, Gabbatha. And it was the preparation of the passover, and about the sixth hour: and he saith unto the Jews, Behold your King! But they cried out, Away with Him, away with Him, crucify Him. Pilate saith unto them, Shall I crucify your King? The chief priests answered, We have no king but Caesar'' (John 18:28 – 19:15).

In the Scripture just preceding these passages, Jesus had gone into the Garden of Gethsemane where He loved to pray. It was to Gethsemane, then, that Judas led the band of men and officers from the chief priests and Pharisees, and betrayed Jesus for thirty pieces of silver—the price of a common slave.

Jesus was arrested and brought before the high priest, who questioned Him and brought Him before Pilate. Pilate then demanded of the Jews, "What *accusation* bring ye against this Man?" In other words, "How does the warrant read? Of what is this Man guilty? What has He done? Why have you had Him arrested, and why are you demanding His death?"

Their accusation was fourfold. They said:

1. *"If He were not a malefactor, we would not have delivered Him up unto thee" (John 18:30).*

Webster defines a *malefactor* as "an evildoer, a criminal." These men who demanded the death of Jesus, declaring that He was an evildoer and a criminal, had witnessed His life. They had followed Him from the very outset of His public ministry; they were no doubt present when He was baptized and when He performed His first miracle at the marriage feast in Cana. They had seen Him heal the sick, open the eyes of the blind, cleanse the lepers, raise the dead, and feed the hungry. They had heard His invitation, "Come unto me, all ye that labour and are heavy laden, and I will give you rest" (Matt. 11:28), and they knew that those who *came* to Him did find healing and rest. They had witnessed His life-giving power—not only in the physical realm, but in the spiritual realm as well. They were in the synagogue when He opened the book of Isaiah and read, "The Spirit of the Lord is upon me, because He hath anointed me to preach the Gospel to the poor; He hath sent me to heal the broken-hearted, to preach deliverance to the captives, and recovering of sight to the blind, to set at liberty them that are bruised, to preach the acceptable year of the Lord" (Luke 4:18,19).

Jesus preached openly, and God had said, "Amen!" to His preaching on many occasions—through signs and wonders and miracles. On more than one occasion God literally spoke from heaven and acknowledged, "This is my beloved Son, in whom I am well pleased."

Divinity is the only cure for fallen humanity. The leopard cannot change his spots, neither can the natural man cleanse himself from sin. The Christ of God, the sacrificial Lamb without spot or blemish, does not simply "patch up" humanity—but through His precious, atoning blood He pardons and redeems those who receive Him, and makes them new creatures: "Therefore if any man be in Christ, he is a new creature: old things are passed away; behold, all things are become new" (II Cor. 5:17). Such was the case of the demoniac of Gadara (Luke 8: 26–39); such was the case of blind Bartimaeus (Mark 10: 46–52); such was the case of the paralyzed man at the pool of Bethesda (John 5:1–15), and scores of others. The chief priests and elders knew this, yet they demanded His death and said to Pilate, "If He were not a malefactor, a criminal and an evildoer, we would not have arrested Him and brought Him to you to be condemned to death!"

Never has any man (or group of men) spoken greater falsehood. Every accusation they brought against Him was false. Jesus Christ, the only begotten Son of God, left the bosom of the Father (John 1:18) and was made a little lower than the angels for the suffering of death, that He might taste death for every man (Heb. 2:9, 14, 15). He lived in a body like unto our bodies (sin apart), and what

88

man could not do because of the weakness of the flesh, what the *law* could not do because of the weakness of the flesh, *Jesus did* so completely and fully that God highly exalted Him and gave Him a name "which is above every name: that at the name of Jesus every knee should bow, of things in heaven, and things in earth, and things under the earth; and that every tongue should confess that Jesus Christ is Lord, to the glory of God the Father" (Phil. 2: 9–11). Because of the perfection of His finished work, He is now seated in the highest seat of heaven at the right hand of the Majesty (Heb. 1:1–3).

These men who accused Jesus the Son of God before Pilate had one day stood on the sidelines at one of His street meetings, and had heard Him declare, "When ye have lifted up the Son of man, then shall ye know that I am He, and that I do nothing of myself; but as my Father hath taught me, I speak these things. And He that sent me is with me: the Father hath not left me alone; for I do always those things that please Him" (John 8:28,29).

In John 17:1–4 Jesus prayed, "Father, the hour is come; glorify thy Son, that thy Son also may glorify thee: As thou hast given Him power over all flesh, that He should give eternal life to as many as thou hast given Him. And this is life eternal, that they might know thee the only true God, and Jesus Christ, whom thou hast sent. I have glorified thee on the earth: I have finished the work which thou gavest me to do."

This was the Man who stood before Pilate while the chief priests, the scribes, and the elders demanded His death. Mark 15:10 tells us that Pilate knew the Jews had brought Jesus to trial because of envy: therefore the question, "What accusation bring ye against this Man?"

2.   *"We have a law, and by our law He ought to die,*

because He made Himself the Son of God" (John 19:7).

Jesus did not *need* to "make" Himself the Son of God. It is true that on occasion He testified that He came from God, but even this was not necessary, because the night He was born the heavens announced His identity:

"And (Mary) brought forth her firstborn son, and wrapped Him in swaddling clothes, and laid Him in a manger; because there was no room for them in the inn. And there were in the same country shepherds abiding in the field, keeping watch over their flock by night. And, lo, the angel of the Lord came upon them, and the glory of the Lord shone round about them: and they were sore afraid. And the angel said unto them, Fear not: for, behold, *I bring you good tidings of great joy, which shall be to all people. For unto you is born this day in the city of David a Saviour, which is Christ the Lord.* And this shall be a sign unto you: Ye shall find the babe wrapped in swaddling clothes, lying in a manger.

"And suddenly there was with the angel a multitude of the heavenly host praising God, and saying, Glory to God in the highest, and on earth peace, good will toward men. And it came to pass, as the angels were gone away from them into heaven, the shepherds said one to another, Let us now go even unto Bethlehem, and see this thing which is come to pass, *which the Lord hath made known unto us.*

"And they came with haste, and found Mary, and Joseph, and the babe lying in a manger. And when they had seen it, *they made known abroad the saying which was told them concerning this child.* And all they that heard it wondered at those things which were told them by the shepherds.

"But Mary kept all these things, and pondered them in her heart. And the shepherds returned, glorifying and praising God for all the things that they had heard and seen, as it was told unto them" (Luke 2:7–20).

No, Jesus did not need to announce that He was God's

Son! The angel of the Lord announced it, and the heavenly host sang about it when He was born. But that was not the only time God proclaimed Jesus as His Son. Let us call Matthew to witness:

John the Baptist was having great revival in Judaea. He was preaching, "Repent ye: for the kingdom of heaven is at hand. For this is he that was spoken of by the prophet Esaias, saying, The voice of one crying in the wilderness, Prepare ye the way of the Lord, make His paths straight. . . Then went out to him Jerusalem, and all Judaea, and all the region round about Jordan, and were baptized of him in Jordan, confessing their sins" (Matt. 3:1–6 in part).

The *Pharisees* saw what was taking place, and together with the Sadducees they came to John and requested baptism; but John was God's preacher, and to him these men looked more like snakes than lambs; so he said to them, "O generation of vipers, who hath warned *you* to flee from the wrath to come? Bring forth therefore fruits meet for repentance . . . I indeed baptize you with water unto repentance: but He that cometh after me is mightier than I, whose shoes I am not worthy to bear: He shall baptize you with the Holy Ghost, and with fire: Whose fan is in His hand, and He will throughly purge His floor, and gather His wheat into the garner; but He will burn up the chaff with unquenchable fire" (Matt. 3:7–12).

John did not baptize the Pharisees and Sadducees because their works did not show forth true repentance. The fruit they bore testified that they were vipers, not sheep. Then one day *Jesus* came to Jordan to be baptized of John:

"Then cometh Jesus from Galilee to Jordan unto John, to be baptized of him. But John forbad Him, saying, I have

91

need to be baptized of thee, and comest thou to me? And Jesus answering said unto him, Suffer it to be so now: for thus it becometh us to fulfil all righteousness. Then he suffered Him.

"And Jesus, when He was baptized, went up straightway out of the water: and, lo, the heavens were opened unto Him, and He saw the Spirit of God descending like a dove, and lighting upon Him: *And lo A VOICE FROM HEAVEN, SAYING, This is my beloved Son, in whom I am well pleased*" (Matt. 3:13–17).

The Pharisees and the Sadducees were there, they witnessed the multitudes that came to be baptized of John, they heard the Voice from heaven when *Jesus* was baptized; therefore they had no excuse for not knowing who He was! It was not needful that Jesus say, "I and my Father are one," because the Father had already said, "*This is my beloved Son.*"

In John 3:1,2 we read, "There was a man of the Pharisees, named Nicodemus, *a ruler of the Jews*: The same came to Jesus by night, and said unto Him, *Rabbi, we KNOW that thou art a teacher come from God: for no man* can do these miracles that thou doest, except God be with him."

Peter, James, and John were with Jesus on the Mount of Transfiguration when Moses and Elijah came down and talked with Him. Peter said, "Lord, it is good for us to be here: if thou wilt, let us make here three tabernacles; one for thee, and one for Moses, and one for Elias." But "while he yet spake, behold, a bright cloud overshadowed them: and behold a voice out of the cloud, which said, THIS IS MY BELOVED SON, IN WHOM I AM WELL PLEASED; HEAR YE HIM. And when the disciples heard it, they fell on their face, and were sore afraid" (Matt. 17:1–6 in part). This is the third time the identity of

Jesus was announced from heaven.

Throughout His earthly ministry He continued to heal the sick, open the eyes of the blind, cleanse the lepers, and raise the dead; and one day toward the end of His earthly sojourn, realizing that His crucifixion was fast approaching, He said, "Now is my soul troubled; and what shall I say? Father, save me from this hour: but for this cause came I unto this hour. Father, glorify thy name. *THEN CAME THERE A VOICE FROM HEAVEN, SAYING, I have both glorified it, and will glorify it again. The people therefore, THAT STOOD BY, AND HEARD IT,* said that it thundered: others said, An angel spake to Him. Jesus answered and said, This voice came not because of me, but for your sakes" (John 12:27–30).

In addition to His miracles, His preaching, and His teaching, here is the fourth recorded account of God Almighty announcing from heaven that Jesus was truly His beloved Son, yea, very God in flesh. Someone has said, "It is unbelievable that the Jews should have missed their Messiah, He was born with so many labels on Him." Scores of prophecies recorded in the Old Testament (and known by the chief priests, scribes, and elders) were fulfilled at His birth and during His ministry; but in spite of it all, they cried out to Pilate, "Crucify Him! Crucify Him! He is an evildoer, a criminal. He made Himself the Son of God, and He ought to die!"

3. *"He is a blasphemer!"*

Matthew tells us that when Jesus was taken before the high priest, the priests, elders, and all the council sought false witnesses against Him, seeking to put Him to death. They questioned Him, but "Jesus held His peace." Then the high priest charged Him, "I adjure thee by the living God, that thou tell us whether thou be the

93

Christ, the Son of God. Jesus saith unto him, Thou hast said: nevertheless I say unto you, Hereafter shall ye see the Son of man sitting on the right hand of power, and coming in the clouds of heaven. Then the high priest rent his clothes, saying, HE HATH SPOKEN BLASPHEMY; what further need have we of witnesses? Behold, now ye have HEARD His blasphemy. What think ye? *They answered and said, He is guilty of death*!'' (Matt. 26:57–68). Read also John 10:32,33 and Mark 14:53–65.

In Galatians 4:4 we read that ''when the fulness of the time was come, *GOD sent forth His Son*, made of a woman, made under the law.'' It was GOD who *set forth* His Son (Rom. 3:25), and it was God who declared, ''*This IS my beloved Son*.''

In John 10:37–39 Jesus said, ''If I do not the *works* of my Father, believe me *not*. But if I do, though ye believe not ME, believe the *works*: that ye may know, and believe, that the Father is in me, and I in Him.''

To His own disciples He said, ''I am the way, the truth, and the life . . . If ye had known me, ye should have known my Father also: and from henceforth ye know Him, and have seen Him. . . He that hath seen me hath seen the Father . . . The words that I speak unto you I speak not of myself: but the Father that dwelleth in me, He doeth the works. Believe me that I am in the Father, and the Father in me: or else believe me for the very works' sake'' (John 14:6–11 in part).

Any person—friend or foe, believer or unbeliever—who witnessed the mighty miracles of Jesus, the works He did as He tabernacled among men, would certainly have known that He was more than man. He was not a blasphemer: He was exactly what God the Father declared Him to be—the only begotten Son of God, the Word in flesh, tabernacling among men. He was Truth, and every word He uttered was truth. His words were spirit and life (John 6:63). He was with the Father in the beginning, He proceeded *from* the Father, He returned *to* the Father, and He is now seated at the Father's right hand.

4.   *"He is perverting the nation, and forbidding to give tribute to Caesar, saying that He Himself is Christ a King" (Luke 23:2).*

Notice that the accusation here is threefold—perverting the nation, forbidding to give tribute to Caesar, and claiming to be a king. Jesus came to *save* the nation Israel, but they rejected Him. Certainly He did not forbid paying tribute to Caesar. In Matthew 22:15–22 we are told that the Pharisees, attempting to "entangle Him in His talk," asked Jesus, "What thinkest thou? Is it lawful to give tribute unto Caesar, or not? But Jesus perceived their wickedness, and said, Why tempt ye me, ye hypocrites? Shew me the tribute money. And they brought unto Him a penny. And He said unto them, Whose is this image and superscription? They say unto Him, Caesar's. Then saith He unto them, *Render therefore unto Caesar the things which are Caesar's; and unto God the things that are God's.* When they had heard these words, they marvelled, and left Him, and went their way."

We know Jesus paid *taxes*, because Matthew 17:24–27 records the fact that when Peter was questioned as to whether or not his Master paid tribute, Jesus told Peter to go to the sea, "and cast an hook, and take up the fish that first cometh up; and when thou hast opened his mouth, thou shalt find a piece of money: that take, and give unto them for me and thee." He did not "pervert the nation" nor did He forbid paying tribute to Caesar.

When Pilate asked Jesus, "*Art* thou the King of the

Jews?" Jesus replied, "Sayest thou this thing of thyself, or did others tell it thee of me?" Pilate then asked, "*Am I a Jew?* Thine *own nation* and the chief priests have delivered thee unto me: *what hast thou done?*" Jesus then explained, "My kingdom is not of this world: if my kingdom were of this world, then would my servants fight, that I should not be delivered to the Jews: but now is my kingdom not from hence" (John 18:33—36).

When Pilate again asked Him, "Art thou a king then?" Jesus simply replied, "To this end was I born." He did not declare that He was king. He said He was *born* to be king of the Jews, He *offered* Himself to them as their Saviour, Messiah, and King; but they rejected Him. They declared, "We will not have this Man to reign over us! We have no king but Caesar!" and they demanded His death.

Jesus presented the truth to the people, He offered them peace — and all who heard Him in faith *received* peace —"peace that passeth understanding." His followers were living epistles, living testimonies that He *did* give peace and life and joy.

In Luke 23:4—12 we read, "Then said Pilate to the chief priests and to the people, I find no fault in this Man. And they were the more fierce, saying, He stirreth up the people, teaching throughout all Jewry, beginning from Galilee to this place. When Pilate heard of Galilee, he asked whether the Man were a Galilaean. And as soon as he knew that He belonged unto Herod's jurisdiction, he sent Him to Herod, who himself also was at Jerusalem at that time.

"And when Herod saw Jesus, he was exceeding glad: for he was desirous to see Him of a long season, because he had heard many things of Him; and he hoped to have seen some miracle done by Him.

"Then he questioned with (Jesus) in many words;

96

but He answered him nothing. And the chief priests and scribes stood and vehemently accused Him. And Herod with his men of war set Him at nought, and mocked Him, and arrayed Him in a gorgeous robe, and sent Him again to Pilate. And the same day Pilate and Herod were made friends together: for before they were at enmity between themselves."

Pilate, a shrewd lawyer, examined Jesus, cross-examined Him, and examined Him again—and then said to the accusers, "I find no fault in this Man touching those things whereof ye accuse Him: No, nor yet Herod: for I sent you to him; and, lo, nothing worthy of death is done unto Him." Thus still declaring Jesus to be faultless, Pilate would have released Him and let Him go — but "they were instant with loud voices, requiring that He might be crucified. *And the voices of them and of the chief priests prevailed. And Pilate gave sentence that it should be as they required.* And he released unto them him that for sedition and murder was cast into prison, whom they had desired; but he delivered Jesus to their will. And as they led Him away, they laid hold upon one Simon, a Cyrenian, coming out of the country, and on him they laid the cross, that he might bear it after Jesus" (Luke 23:13–26).

There was not one word of truth in any accusation brought against Jesus by His own people. Every accusation was false; but in spite of this, and in spite of the fact that Pilate found no fault in Him, "they cried out the more, saying, Let Him be crucified! When Pilate saw that he could prevail nothing, but that rather a tumult was made, he took water, and washed His hands before the multitude, saying, I am innocent of the blood of this just Person: see ye to it. *Then answered all the people, and said, HIS BLOOD BE ON US, AND ON OUR CHILDREN!*" (Matt. 27:23–25).

The Jews spoke these words more than nineteen hundred years ago — and they have suffered a blood-bath such as no other nation has known in the history of mankind! They have been butchered. cremated, slaughtered by the million — and they are still suffering. They asked for it when they said, "Give us Barabbas, crucify JESUS! Let His blood be on us, and on our children!"

What Accusation Bring YE Against Jesus?

Dear reader, are YOU a child of God? Have YOU trusted Jesus as your personal Saviour? If not, what accusation do YOU bring against this Man?

You may say, "Sir, *I am neutral*! I am not a believer, but neither am I an atheist. I am not such a bad *sinner*, either. I am not *for* Jesus, but I am not *against* Him. I am entirely neutral."

According to the words of Jesus, this is an impossibility: In Matthew 12:30 He declared, *"He that is not with me is against me; and he that gathereth not with me scattereth abroad."* There is no such thing as spiritual neutrality. We are either children of God or children of the devil. We are either believers or unbelievers. We are saved — or we are lost. Therefore we are either for Jesus, or we are against Him. We gather people to Him, or we scatter them and drive them from Him.

If you do not love Jesus, if you are not saved and serving Him, what *accusation* do you bring against Him? Let us look at just a few of the accusations brought against Him by men with whom I have dealt personally in the years of my ministry:

1. Some say, *"Salvation is all right for you, sir. You are a minister, so salvation is all right for you and your family; but it is just not for ME!"*

98

Would you accuse Jesus of showing partiality? The Word of God declares that "there is no respect of persons with God" (Rom. 2:11). Would you be guilty of calling God a liar? That is what you are doing if you are saying, "Salvation is all right for others—but not for *me*." The Bible teaches that Jesus died for the whole world, and that God laid on Him the sins of all persons of all ages:

"For God so loved the world, that He gave His only begotten Son, that *whosoever* believeth in Him should not perish, but have everlasting life" (John 3:16). Are *you* in the *world*? If you are, God loved you and gave Jesus to die for you. His love was for the whole world, His invitation is to "whosoever will." You are included. Salvation is for YOU if you will receive Jesus.

"ALL we like sheep have gone astray; we have turned every one to his own way; and the Lord hath laid on Him the iniquity of us ALL" (Isa. 53:6). Notice that this verse of Scripture begins with "ALL" and ends with "ALL." We are all "in the same boat"—born in sin and shapen in iniquity; but God laid our sins on Jesus, and HE nailed them to His cross. You are included in the "ALL." Believe on the Lord Jesus Christ, and He will save you now.

Jesus said, "Come unto me, ALL ye that labour and are heavy laden, and I will give you rest" (Matt. 11:28). The invitation is to ALL—all who labor and are heavy laden can have rest by coming to Jesus. The sinner's part is simply *to come to Him*; the sin-debt has already been paid, salvation has been purchased, and redemption is for you if you will only come to Jesus.

". . . Him that cometh to me I will in no wise cast out" (John 6:37). You are the "him." The promise is to all. Come to Him and He will keep His promise. Under no circumstance will He cast out *anyone* who comes to

Him for salvation.

"The Lord is not slack concerning His promise, as some men count slackness; but is longsuffering to us-ward, *not willing that ANY should perish, but that ALL should come to repentance*" (II Pet. 3:9).

If you say, *"Salvation is not for me,"* you are branding God's Word a lie. It is not God's will that ANY should perish — and certainly that includes YOU. If you spend eternity in the lake of fire it will not be because of God's will; it will be because of your own stubborn will. If you go to hell you will go there because you refused to come to Jesus. Before you reject His loving invitation, consider these solemn, solemn words:

"He that believeth on the Son of God hath the witness in himself: he that believeth NOT God hath made Him a liar; because he believeth not the record that God gave of His Son" (I John 5:10).

Do not accuse Jesus of saving some and rejecting others. Salvation is for all who will come to God in believing faith, trusting Jesus as personal Saviour.

2.   Some say, *"I would LIKE to be saved, I really WANT to be saved, but I cannot understand HOW to be saved."*
If this is the accusation YOU bring against Jesus, I assure you it is false. Sinners are not saved by understanding the *"how"* of salvation, but by believing what God says in His Word:

"God hath chosen the foolish things of the world to confound the wise; and God hath chosen the weak things of the world to confound the things which are mighty; and base things of the world, and things which are despised, hath God chosen, yea, and things which are not, to bring to nought things that are: that no flesh should glory in

100

His presence. *But of HIM are ye in Christ Jesus, who of God is made unto us wisdom, and righteousness, and sanctification, and redemption: That, according as it is written, He that glorieth, let him glory in the Lord*" (I Cor. 1:27–31).

Thus we see that the very wisdom and *ability to receive Jesus* is the gift of God! When we receive Christ, *He* becomes our righteousness, our wisdom, our holiness, our sanctification, our redemption. "For by GRACE are ye saved through FAITH; and that not of yourselves: it is the gift of God" (Eph. 2:8). Grace is God's unmerited, unearned, undeserved favor to man. God's grace saves us, but grace becomes ours by faith; and the very faith through which we trust Jesus is also a gift of God (Rom. 10:17; John 5:24; I Pet. 1:23).

` Salvation is God's *gift* – it is not of works, nor of understanding. It comes simply by receiving Jesus, simply believing what God has said in His Word. If God says it, it is truth, because God cannot lie (Heb. 6:18; Tit. 1:2). Salvation is not by works, it is not by righteous living. We are saved by God's grace, according to His mercy – not by *understanding*, but by accepting what God offers. Hear the Word, believe and receive the Word, and God will "born" you into the family of heaven.

3. Some say, "I believe I *could* be saved, and I think I know *how* to be saved; *but I could never live the Christian life.*"

If this is the accusation *you* bring against Jesus, it, too, is false. The God who so loved us that He provided salvation for us through His only begotten Son, has also provided *victory* for us. He has made us *more* than conquerors:

"What shall we then say to these things? If God be

101

for us, who can be against us? . . . Who shall separate us from the love of Christ? Shall tribulation, or distress, or persecution, or famine, or nakedness, or peril, or sword? As it is written, For thy sake we are killed all the day long; we are accounted as sheep for the slaughter. *Nay, in all these things we are MORE than conquerors through Him that loved us.* For I am persuaded, that neither death, nor life, nor angels, nor principalities, nor powers, nor things present, nor things to come, nor height, nor depth, nor any other creature, shall be able to separate us from the love of God, which is in Christ Jesus our Lord'' (Rom. 8:31, 35–39).

One of the most precious promises in all of the Bible is I Corinthians 10:13:

"There hath no temptation taken you but such as is common to man: BUT GOD IS FAITHFUL, who will not suffer you to be tempted above that ye are able; but will with the temptation also make a way to escape, that ye may be able to bear it."

Read this verse, re-read it, memorize it. And please notice, there can no temptation come upon *you* but such as is common to *all* men. Notice also that it is GOD who is faithful, it is GOD who will not permit you to be tempted above what you can bear, it is GOD who makes a way of escape for you. Never again say that you cannot live the Christian life. You CAN — if you will believe on the Lord Jesus Christ and allow HIM to take up His abode in your heart: ". . . for He hath said, I will never leave thee, nor forsake thee. So that we may boldly say, The Lord is my helper, and I will not fear what man shall do unto me!'' (Heb. 13:5,6).

4. There are those who say, "I believe I could be saved, and I think I understand the plan of salvation; perhaps

102

I could even live the Christian life — *but there is just too much to GIVE UP in order to become a Christian."* Is that *your* accusation? If it is, I suggest you visit the jail in your city, visit the chain gang, go to the state penitentiary and ask the warden to let you talk with the men who sit in the little gray cells a few steps from the electric chair or the gas chamber. Ask *them* what *they* have given up to be *sinners!*

Now hear the words of Jesus: "For whosoever will save his life shall lose it: and whosoever will lose his life for my sake shall find it. *For what is a man profited, if he shall gain the whole world, and lose his own soul? or what shall a man give in exchange for his soul?"* (Matt. 16:25,26).

Suppose you became dictator of the whole wide world and came into possession of all the *wealth* of all the world. You would gain all this earth holds — and yet, if you died without faith in the shed blood of Jesus, it would be better for you if you had never been born! What, indeed, shall it profit a man if he shall *gain* the whole world *and lose his own soul?*

Remember, beloved: we are not saved by *"giving up,"* but by *receiving*. It is true that when the unbeliever hears the Gospel and believes on the Lord Jesus Christ as Saviour, sinful habits fall away and that person no longer loves the things of the world; but JESUS gives possessions so much better than anything earth can dream of! He gives joy unspeakable and full of glory, He gives peace that surpasses all understanding, He gives rest to the weary soul — and He gives an eternal home in heaven. To His own He promised, "Let not your heart be troubled: ye believe in God, believe also in me. In my Father's house are many mansions: if it were not so, I would have told you. *I go*

103

to prepare a place for YOU. And if I go and prepare a place for you, I will come again, and receive you unto myself; that where I am, there ye may be also" (John 14:1–3).

For nineteen hundred years Jesus has been preparing that glorious place for His children. If you will study Revelation chapter 21 you will find a description of that Pearly White City where the born again ones will dwell forever. Paul tells us, "Eye hath not seen, nor ear heard, neither have entered into the heart of man, the things which God hath prepared for them that love Him" (I Cor. 2:9). It is a human impossibility to imagine what heaven is like. God will give us a glorified body like the glorified body of Jesus — for without such a body we could not enter that city; we would be consumed by its brightness. Just as *God* prepared salvation for us, *Jesus* is preparing a home in heaven for us.

Too much to give up in order to be a Christian? Listen to this:

"Blessed be the God and Father of our Lord Jesus Christ, which according to His abundant mercy hath begotten us again unto a lively hope by the resurrection of Jesus Christ from the dead, to an inheritance incorruptible, and undefiled, and that fadeth not away, reserved in heaven for you, who are kept by the power of God through faith unto salvation ready to be revealed in the last time" (I Pet. 1:3–5).

If you are *saved*, bow your knees and worship the Lord. Thank Him and praise Him for saving you.

If you are NOT saved, stop making false accusations and *believe* on Him — trust Him NOW. Let Jesus come into your heart this moment. He will save you — and you will know it.

I join Pilate in declaring, "I find no fault in Jesus!"

104

"WILT THOU BE MADE WHOLE?"

"WILT THOU BE MADE WHOLE?"

"After this there was a feast of the Jews; and Jesus went up to Jerusalem. Now there is at Jerusalem by the sheep market a pool, which is called in the Hebrew tongue Bethesda, having five porches. In these lay a great multitude of impotent folk, of blind, halt, withered, waiting for the moving of the water. For an angel went down at a certain season into the pool, and troubled the water: whosoever then first after the troubling of the water stepped in was made whole of whatsoever disease he had.

"And a certain man was there, which had an infirmity thirty and eight years. When Jesus saw him lie, and knew that he had been now a long time in that case, He saith unto him, Wilt thou be made whole? The impotent man answered Him, Sir, I have no man, when the wat r is troubled, to put me into the pool: but while I am coming, another steppeth down before me.

"Jesus saith unto him, Rise, take up thy bed, and walk. And immediately the man was made whole, and took up his bed, and walked: and on the same day was the sabbath. The Jews therefore said unto him that was cured, It is the sabbath day: it is not lawful for thee to carry thy bed. He answered them, He that made me whole, the same said unto me, Take up thy bed, and walk. Then asked they him, What man is that which said unto thee, Take up thy bed, and walk? And he that was healed wist not who it was: for Jesus had conveyed Himself away, a multitude being in that place.

"Afterward Jesus findeth him in the temple, and said unto him, Behold, thou art made whole: sin no more, lest a worse thing come unto thee. The man departed, and told the Jews that it was Jesus, which had made him whole. And therefore did the Jews persecute Jesus, and sought to slay Him, because He had done these things on the sabbath day" (John 5:1-16).

Our Scripture begins, "*After this . . . .*" After *what*?

Let us look at some of the incidents immediately preceding this miracle performed by Jesus at the pool of Bethesda:

In John chapter 4 He traveled into Galilee, going by way of Samaria. He stopped at Jacob's well to rest, and a woman came to the well to draw water. Jesus asked her for a drink, in the course of the conversation she was saved, and a great revival broke out among the Samaritans. Many of them believed on Jesus and were saved.

He then came again into Cana of Galilee where He had performed His first miracle at the wedding supper. In Cana there was a certain nobleman who lived in Capernaum and whose son was at the point of death. "When he heard that Jesus was come out of Judaea into Galilee, he went unto Him, and besought Him that He would come down, and heal his son. . . Then said Jesus unto him, Except ye see signs and wonders, ye will not believe." The nobleman then simply said, "Sir, come down *ere my child die!*" In other words, he said, "Jesus, unless *you* heal my child he is sure to die." Jesus answered him, "Go thy way; thy son liveth" — that is, "If you sincerely believe in your heart that I am the last hope of your child, if you sincerely believe that I can heal him, *go home*. Your son is well!" The man believed what Jesus said, and the next day he returned to his home; but before he reached the house his servants met him and said to him, *"Thy son liveth."* When the nobleman inquired as to what hour the child was healed, his servants told him, *"YESTERDAY AT THE SEVENTH HOUR the fever left him*. So the father knew that it was *AT THE SAME HOUR, IN THE WHICH JESUS SAID UNTO HIM, Thy son liveth: and himself believed, and his whole house."* You can read the entire account in John 4:46—54.

It was *"after this"* that Jesus traveled up to Jerusalem at the time of a feast of the Jews—probably the feast of

108

Pentecost. The Jewish religion called for the observance of many holy days, holidays, and feasts. Near the temple in Jerusalem was a sheep market—a place where lambs were sold to be offered in the religious ceremonies in the temple. Thus in the course of a year tens of thousands of people came to the sheep market to purchase animals for sacrifice.

Near the sheep market was the pool of Bethesda, a pool surrounded by five porches in which lay a great multitude of sick people—blind, halt, withered, waiting for the mysterious moving of the water in the pool. Now here is a picture we need to see today: Jerusalem was the Holy City, the city of worship. The temple was there—but these sick folk were not around the altar in the temple; they were in the five porches around the pool of Bethesda. *Yet this pool was only a stone's cast from the temple area.* WHY were the sick people around the pool instead of being in the temple where the healing and saving power of God *should be* experienced by poor souls in need? The answer is evident:

At the time when Jesus came into the world to offer Himself to His own people as their Messiah, the temple services were nothing more than dead, formal, religious rituals; the Power had departed. Therefore if those who needed healing expected to *receive* that healing by the power of God, they knew they must find it somewhere outside the dead ceremonies of the temple.

I am afraid we have more form than Spirit today! Sad but true, all too often needy souls have lost confidence in the church—which *should* be the place in the community where sinners go to seek the Saviour and to meet God in satisfying, healing, delivering power. But today too many churches have become places of ceremony and dead formalism, "having a *form* of godliness, but denying the *power* thereof" (II Tim. 3:5).

Notice the three classifications of sick folk mentioned as lying in the five porches around the pool: There were the *"blind,"* the *"halt,"* the *"withered"* — all of which portray the unbeliever. The sinner is blind—blinded by the god of this age "lest the light of the glorious Gospel of Christ, who is the image of God, should shine unto (him)" (II Cor. 4:3,4). The sinner is halt and withered, crippled by sin. There is no life in him: "She that liveth in pleasure is dead while she liveth" (I Tim. 5:6). Now a blind person *knows* that he cannot see, he recognizes his blindness. Likewise, a crippled, withered person knows his condition. Thus the multitude of blind, halt, and withered people in the porches around the pool of Bethesda were there because they knew they had a need. They were waiting for the moving of the water in the pool.

I think most of us—even we who are full time Christian workers—would be surprised if we really knew how many unsaved people are waiting, hoping, trusting that someone will invite them to church or instruct them in the way of salvation. Seemingly, the whole world has gone after the devil—but there is a hunger in the hearts of the multitudes. They are hungry to know the way of salvation. True, there are those who are haughty and stubborn, who are determined to go on in the way of sin and who stedfastly refuse to hear the Gospel; but there are also multitudes of poor, spiritually blind, spiritually crippled people who, like those around the pool of Bethesda, are *just waiting.*

The Scripture tells us that these people were *"waiting for the moving of the water,* for an angel went down at a certain season into the pool, and troubled the water." *Water* is used in the Bible as a type of the Word of God. In John 4:13,14 Jesus said to the Samaritan woman, "Whosoever drinketh of this water shall thirst again: but whosoever

110

drinketh of the water that I shall give him shall never thirst; but the water that I shall give him shall be in him a well of water springing up into everlasting life." The woman at the well requested "living water," and Jesus gave it to her. What did He give her? She said, "I know that Messias cometh, which is called Christ," and Jesus said to her, "I THAT SPEAK UNTO THEE AM HE." Seven words — but the woman heard those words, she believed the Word, and an artesian well of living water bubbled up within her soul! The "water" is the Word. In John 15:3 Jesus said to His disciples, *"Now ye are clean through the WORD which I have spoken unto you."*

Dirty, filthy sinners are made clean by the Word—the Word of God which is "the *power* of God unto salvation to every one that believeth" (Rom. 1:16).

In. Ephesians 5:25 and 26 we are told that Christ loved the Church and gave Himself for it, "that He might sanctify and cleanse it *with the washing of water by the Word.*"

Notice, in our Scripture text the moving of the water came from heaven: an angel came down at a "certain season" and troubled the water. There is not much "troubling of the water" today. It is true that we have more preaching today than ever before, we have more Sunday schools and more churches than we have ever had; but the present day churches are trying to trouble the waters through methods other than the preaching of the Word of God. Liberalism and modernism have been substituted for the Gospel. But there is only *one way* to trouble the waters and bring healing power to the souls of poor, blind, halt, withered sinners, and that is the method used by Paul in I Corinthians 15:1–4.

In verse 4 of our text there are three things I would like to point out:

1.   The water was troubled *"at a certain season."*

2. *"Whosoever"* — king or peasant, rich or poor, master or slave—stepped into the pool first after the troubling of the water was instantaneously made whole —

3. *". . . of WHATSOEVER disease he had!"*

Any and all persons could be healed of any and all diseases — but the healing power was present *only* AT THE "CERTAIN SEASON." There are those who say, "I will be saved when I am *ready* to be saved, when I have made things right, when I have paid up all my debts and apologized to all the people I have wronged, when I feel that I can live as a Christian *should* live." Friend, if that is what you are saying, I beg you in the name of Jesus never to say it again! You will *not* be saved when you "get ready" to be saved: You will be saved when the Holy Spirit of God troubles your soul through the Word of God (the living water). Jesus said, "No man can come to me, except the Father which hath sent me *draw* him . . ." (John 6:44).

It is true that "whosoever shall call upon the name of the Lord shall be saved"—but it is also true that they cannot call on Him in whom they have not believed, they cannot believe in Him of whom they have not heard, they cannot hear without a preacher, "and how shall they preach except they be sent? . . . *So then faith cometh by hearing, and hearing by the Word of God*" (Rom. 10:13–17). Saving faith comes by hearing the Word of God; and it is the plan and program of God that ministers are sent to *preach* the Word, the needy sinner *hears* the Word, believes the Word, and then calls upon the name of the Lord, and God saves him.

At the pool of Bethesda God sent an angel to trouble the water. In these present days He calls and ordains ministers and sends them to trouble the water by preaching the Word. It is through "the foolishness of preaching" that God saves whosoever hears and believes the Word (I Cor. 1:21;

112

John 5:24; I Pet. 1:23; James 1:21).

My precious friend, if you are not born again, is this *your* "certain season"? Has this message troubled the waters of your soul? Have you been made to realize that you are spiritually blind, crippled, withered, and dead in trespasses and sin? If the Word of God has troubled your heart through this message, then this IS your "certain season" and I pray that you will receive Jesus NOW. You are among the "whosoever," no matter what your sin may be. The precious blood of Jesus cleanses from "whatsoever" – but only when the Spirit calls. If this is the season for you, please do not turn Him away. Let Jesus come into your heart by faith, trust Him, and He will save you now:

". . . If thou shalt confess with thy mouth the Lord Jesus, and shalt believe in thine heart that God hath raised Him from the dead, thou shalt be saved. For with the heart man believeth unto righteousness; and with the mouth confession is made unto salvation" (Rom. 10:9,10).

Verse 5 of our text tells us that *"a certain man was there."* This man, one of the multitude lying in the porches around the pool, had been paralyzed for thirty-eight years. How many of those years had been spent at the pool, we do not know. There is reason to believe that he had been there many, many years, because in verse 6 we are told that Jesus *knew* that he had been there a long time. Think of it! This man had had an infirmity for almost forty years, and in that time he had been totally dependent upon others. Many of those years he had lain near the pool of Bethesda, just inside the gate where tens of thousands of worshippers must of necessity pass by in purchasing lambs for the temple sacrifices. Year after year they came to the sheep market, purchased their sacrificial animal, and walked past the pool; yet if they saw the multitude of poor, blind, crippled

113

folk they had no time to help them, they had no compassion on them.

The same is true today: Tens of thousands of church members — and that includes some preachers — are so busy with the program of their denomination and the religious activities of their own church that they have no time to give to poor, blind, crippled sinners—withered souls waiting for someone to love them and invite them to the house of God or tell them how to be saved!

"*When Jesus saw him. . . .*" No soul in need escaped the eyes of Jesus! From His baptism until He cried out from the cross, "Father, forgive them, they know not what they do," He was seeking and saving souls. He was never too busy, never in such a hurry that He did not have time for those who needed help. It was only natural that when He came to Jerusalem to visit the temple, His eyes were searching and His heart was longing for some precious, needy soul who was willing to accept His help.

"Wilt Thou Be Made Whole?"

The impotent man replied, "*Sir, I have no man, when the water is troubled, to put me into the pool: but while I am coming, another steppeth down before me.*" This is one of the saddest statements ever to fall from the lips of man! This poor paralytic was not on "skid row," he was not on the street of forgotten men, he was not at the door of a theatre, a dancehall, or a nightclub. He was lying within a stone's throw of the *temple*, the place where thousands of "religious" people went to worship. Year after year they had passed him by, and in answer to the Lord's question he replied, "I have no man to help me!"

Fellow believer, who helped YOU to find the way of salvation? Did no one pray for you? Did no one invite you

114

to church or give you a little Gospel tract? If you will honestly consider, I believe you will admit that you DO know someone who prayed for you, someone who witnessed to you, someone—perhaps more than *one* person—who helped you to find the way of salvation. If ten thousand people were gathered into one group, every one of them born again Christians, and I should ask them, "How many of you were saved entirely apart from human help—no one invited you to church, no one prayed for you, no one gave you the plan of salvation?" I do not believe one single, solitary soul would lift a hand and say, "I found the way of salvation and was saved entirely without the help of any man!"

Do not misunderstand me — we cannot save souls, we cannot even *convict* souls, much less forgive their sins; but we are commanded to let our light shine before the world, we are commanded to go and teach, preach, and witness. As Christians it is our duty to tell others about the wonderful Saviour who saved US from sin. In James 5:20 we read, "Let him know, that he which converteth the sinner from the error of his way shall save a soul from death, and shall hide a multitude of sins." You will notice this does not say, "he which *saves* the sinner," but "he which *converteth* the sinner *from the error of his way.*" When we invite sinners to hear the Gospel by which the new birth comes, when we cause unbelievers to turn to Jesus and be converted from a life of sin by putting their faith in the shed blood of the Son of God, then we have definitely had a part in bringing them to salvation. They are saved from eternal death, and a multitude of sins are covered by the blood of Jesus.

In this Dispensation of Grace it has pleased God to allow you and me to be witnesses for Him, to tell others of the saving power of Jesus, and to cause men to become thirsty for the water of life. Jesus told His disciples, "Ye are the salt of the earth . . . Ye are the light of the world." We should be "salty" Christians and cause others to thirst after God. We should keep our lamps ever trimmed and burning, pointing weary sinners to the Light of the world, the Lord Jesus Christ.

It is a grand and glorious privilege to be a child of God – but just so grand and glorious the privilege, so grave the responsibility. In Ezekiel 3:18,19 God says, "When I say unto the wicked, Thou shalt surely die; and thou givest him not warning, nor speakest to warn the wicked from his wicked way, to save his life; the same wicked man shall die in his iniquity; *but his blood will I require at thine hand.* Yet if thou warn the wicked, and he turn not from his wickedness, nor from his wicked way, he shall die in his iniquity; *but thou hast delivered thy soul!*" God help us not to pass by on the other side, allowing those who need the Lord to die in their sin and be eternally lost! Many are waiting for the moving of the water. We can help them to find Jesus.

The Scripture tells us that there was a "multitude" of impotent folk in the porches around the pool of Bethesda, but our attention is called to *"a certain man"* who caught the eye of Jesus. There is a lesson here for us: *God does not expect us to win the world by ourselves,* but there is a certain man, a certain person somewhere, whom God wants us to win. A believer should not go to heaven without being the instrument in the hand of God to lead *some other person* to heaven. Somewhere there is "a certain man" (or "a certain woman") whom God wants us to see and win for Christ.

"Rise, Take Up Thy Bed, and Walk!"

Certainly from the human standpoint a man who had been paralyzed for thirty-eight years would have answered,

116

"I cannot rise, I cannot take up my bed, I cannot *walk*! Can you not see that my limbs are stiff, wasted, and useless? Why do you say to me, 'Rise and walk'?" From the standpoint of human reasoning this man had a perfect right to argue with Jesus — but that is where *faith* comes in. The man knew his condition and he was at the pool because he wanted to be *delivered* from that condition. It does not matter whether or not he knew Jesus was the Son of God. He had *faith* in this Man who had just said to him, "Rise, take up thy bed, and walk."

So it is today: We are saved by God's grace through faith. Hearing the Word of God brings faith that *accepts* God's grace even though we cannot understand it. Grace is unmerited, unearned favor. Why should God so love me that He allowed Jesus to die for me? Why should Jesus love me so much that He allowed me to live a wretched, sinful life for many years — and then when I called on His precious name He saved me? We could ask "Why?" over and over and over again — but God does not want us to question. *He wants us to believe His Word* (Eph. 2:8,9; Rom. 10:17).

The man who had been paralyzed for so many years heard the words of Jesus, he believed what he heard, and immediately he was made whole. Immediately he stood up and walked. BY FAITH he stood, he picked up his bed, and he walked.

Living Faith

"For as the body without the spirit is dead, so faith without works is dead also" (James 2:26).

The man who was waiting for "the moving of the water" heard the words, "Rise, take up thy bed, and walk." He did not say, *"I cannot."* At the words of Jesus, he exercised faith by the act of rising; and the split second he

117

put his body in motion to rise, *God honored his faith*, healed his body, and saved his soul!

In verse 13 we read, "And he that was healed wist not who it was: for Jesus had conveyed Himself away . . . ." This man did not know who Jesus was; but a bit later Jesus found him in the temple and said to him, "Behold, thou art made whole: sin no more, lest a worse thing come unto thee." When he learned who had healed him, he believed on Him, trusted Him, and from that moment on he walked in faith. He had exercised *living* faith—faith in God, faith in the Lord Jesus Christ, the faith that brings healing to the soul and supplies grace for every need—physical, spiritual, eternal.

I wonder if I am speaking to some precious sinner who has been paralyzed by sin for thirty-eight years — or longer? Perhaps I am speaking to some *young* person who has been blinded by sin for only a short time. Whatever your age, whatever your condition, remember verse 4: *when the water is troubled*, "whosoever"—young or old, rich or poor, wise or foolish, bond or free, religious sinner or outrageous sinner—can be made whole of "whatsoever" disease (sin, iniquity, wickedness). Regardless of how ungodly you have been or how long you may have lived in sin, "whosoever" you are you can be saved from "whatsoever" you have done —but not WHENSOEVER you choose. It must be at your "certain season," when you hear the Word of God and the Spirit troubles your soul, convicting and drawing you to God. If you reject Jesus and turn a deaf ear to the calling of the Word and the wooing of the Spirit, do not be surprised if one day you hear Him say, "Depart into everlasting fire! I never knew you!" My precious friend, if you are not a born again believer, God grant that this be the "certain season" when you will be healed of your disease of sin, leased from the bondage of the iniquity that blinds you and causes you to be spiritually crippled.

There Is Only One Way to Be Saved

In John 10:1–11 Jesus said, "Verily, verily, I say unto you, He that entereth not by the door into the sheepfold, but climbeth up some other way, the same is a thief and a robber. But he that entereth in by the door is the shepherd of the sheep. To him the porter openeth; and the sheep hear his voice: and he calleth his own sheep by name, and leadeth them out. And when he putteth forth his own sheep, he goeth before them, and the sheep follow him: for they know his voice. And a stranger will they not follow, but will flee from him: for they know not the voice of strangers.

"This parable spake Jesus unto them: but they understood not what things they were which He spake unto them. Then said Jesus unto them again, Verily, verily, I say unto you, I am the Door of the sheep. All that ever came before me are thieves and robbers: but the sheep did not hear them. *I am the Door*: by me if any man enter in, he shall be saved, and shall go in and out, and find pasture. The thief cometh not, but for to steal, and to kill, and to destroy: I am come that they might have life, and that they might have it more abundantly. *I am the Good Shepherd: the Good Shepherd giveth His life for the sheep.*"

There is only one way to heaven. Jesus is the Door, He is the Way TO the door and He is the Truth *about* the door. He gives life that we may enter the door, and no man can come to God except by Jesus Christ.

Jesus is looking your way. If down in your heart you feel the need of a Saviour, this is your season. The Door is open; His arms are outstretched in your direction. *"Believe on the Lord Jesus Christ, and thou shalt be saved"* (Acts 16:31).

119

THE QUESTION THAT CANNOT BE ANSWERED

THE QUESTION
THAT CANNOT BE ANSWERED

"What shall we then say to these things? If God be for us, who can be against us? He that spared not His own Son, but delivered Him up for us all, how shall He not with Him also freely give us all things?

"Who shall lay anything to the charge of God's elect? It is God that justifieth. Who is he that condemneth? It is Christ that died, yea rather, that is risen again, who is even at the right hand of God, who also maketh intercession for us.

"Who shall separate us from the love of Christ? Shall tribulation, or distress, or persecution, or famine, or nakedness, or peril, or sword? As it is written, For thy sake we are killed all the day long; we are accounted as sheep for the slaughter.

"Nay, in all these things we are more than conquerors through Him that loved us. For I am persuaded, that neither death, nor life, nor angels, nor principalities, nor powers, nor things present, nor things to come, nor height, nor depth, nor any other creature, shall be able to separate us from the love of God, which is in Christ Jesus our Lord" (Rom. 8:31–39).

Who Shall Lay Anything to the Charge of God's Elect?

First of all, who ARE the "elect"? The only place to find the right answer is in the Word of God.

In both the Old and New Testaments the Hebrew and Greek words translated "elect" are also rendered "election," "choose," "chosen"—and always the meaning is *to be chosen of God*, or *to choose*. The words are used with reference to Divine choice, and also to *man's* choosing.

In the *Old* Testament era *the nation of Israel* was the

"elect" (Isa. 45:4). In the *New* Testament *the Church of the living God* is the elect.

Paul's letter to the church at Ephesus opens thus: "Paul, an apostle of Jesus Christ by the will of God, to the saints which are at Ephesus, and to the faithful in Christ Jesus: grace be to you, and peace, from God our Father, and from the Lord Jesus Christ. Blessed be the God and Father of our Lord Jesus Christ, who hath blessed us with all spiritual blessings in heavenly places in Christ: *according as He hath CHOSEN US IN HIM before the foundation of the world*, that we should be holy and without blame before Him in love: *having PREDESTINATED us unto the adoption of children by Jesus Christ to Himself, according to the good pleasure of His will*, to the praise of the glory of His grace, wherein He hath made us accepted in the Beloved. In whom we have redemption through His blood, the forgiveness of sins, according to the riches of His grace" (Eph. 1:1–7).

The New Testament Church is the "elect" made up of those who are born again—but this does not mean that some are chosen to be saved while others are elected to be damned. John 3:16 settles this question, with no room whatsoever for doubt: "For God so loved the world, that He gave His only begotten Son, that *whosoever believeth in Him* should not perish, but have everlasting life." God loved *the WORLD*, and He saves whosoever believes on Jesus and receives Him. It is true that the Church *as a BODY* was chosen from the foundation of the world, but *the Church is made up of individuals who choose Jesus*. In Matthew 11:28 Jesus invited, "*Come unto me, ALL ye that labour and are heavy laden,* and I will give you rest." Peter tells us that God is "*not willing that ANY should perish, but that ALL should come to repentance*" (II Pet. 3:9). Therefore we see that "election" does not mean that some persons are elected to be damned while others are elected to be saved.

In this day and age, "the elect" refers to the born again ones who make up the New Testament Church. It is true that election is according to the foreknowledge of God — He knew the end in the beginning, He lives in the eternal present, He is sovereign, He is the great "I AM." But election is wholly and entirely of grace, and apart from grace *no one* could be saved. Human merit has nothing to do with becoming one of the elect. While we were yet sinners God loved us, Christ died for us; the Holy Spirit calls us—and when we hear the Word, receive the Word, and believe on the Lord Jesus Christ, according to the Scriptures we are *saved*. Thus, when Paul asked, "Who shall lay anything to the charge of *God's ELECT*?" he was asking, "Who shall lay anything to the charge of one who belongs to the body of Christ, a born again child of God?"

In the Amplified New Testament we read, "Who shall bring any charge against God's elect (when it is) God who justifies—who puts us in right relation to Himself? (Who shall come forward and accuse or impeach those whom God has chosen? Will God, who acquits us?) Who is there to condemn (us)? Will Christ Jesus, the Messiah, who died, or rather who was raised from the dead, who is at the right hand of God actually pleading as He intercedes for us?"

1. *"Who shall lay anything to the charge of God's elect?"*
    CAN GOD?

The answer to that question follows immediately in the Scripture: "It is GOD that *justifieth*." How does God justify us? We find the answer in Romans 3:21—28:

"But now the righteousness of God without the law is

125

manifested, being witnessed by the law and the prophets; even the righteousness of God which is by faith of Jesus Christ unto all and upon all them that believe: for there is no difference: for all have sinned, and come short of the glory of God; being justified freely by His grace through the redemption that is in Christ Jesus: whom God hath set forth to be a propitiation through faith in His blood, to declare His righteousness for the remission of sins that are past, through the forbearance of God; to declare, I say, at this time His righteousness: *that He might be JUST, and the JUSTIFIER of him which believeth in Jesus.*"

ALL have sinned; therefore ALL are condemned, lost; but the individual who hears the Gospel and believes in the shed blood of Jesus receives the redemption that is IN Christ Jesus. We are justified by faith in His shed blood and His finished work:

"Therefore being justified by faith, we have peace with God through our Lord Jesus Christ: by whom also we have access by faith into this grace wherein we stand, and rejoice in hope of the glory of God. And not only so, but we glory in tribulations also: knowing that tribulation worketh patience; and patience, experience; and experience, hope: and hope maketh not ashamed; because the love of God is shed abroad in our hearts by the Holy Ghost which is given unto us. For when we were yet without strength, in due time Christ died for the ungodly. For scarcely for a righteous man will one die: yet peradventure for a good man some would even dare to die. *BUT GOD* commendeth His love toward us, in that, while we were yet sinners, Christ died for us. Much more then, being now justified by His blood, we shall be saved from wrath through Him. For if, when we were enemies, we were reconciled to God by the death of His Son, much more, being reconciled, we shall

be saved by His life. And not only so, *but we also joy in God through our Lord Jesus Christ, by whom we have now received the atonement*" (Rom. 5:1-11).

It was God who so loved the world that He set forth Jesus to be the Saviour of sinners. It was God who commended His love toward us in that while we were yet sinners He allowed Christ to die that we might be saved; and now God forgives the sinner *for Christ's sake* (Eph. 4:32).

Will GOD lay anything to the charge of His elect, His children who *become* His children through the shed blood and finished work of His only begotten Son? It is God who justifies us and saves us for the *sake* of His dear Son. It is God who makes us fit for the kingdom and accepts us into His family. *Would He then condemn us*? Since God IS God, righteous and holy, *He cannot* lay anything to the charge of those who have exercised faith in the shed blood of Jesus, those who are covered by the blood, accepted in the Beloved, saved for Christ's sake and therefore *complete* in Jesus:

"*For IN HIM dwelleth all the fulness of the Godhead bodily. And ye are complete in Him, which is the head of all principality and power*" *(Col. 2:9,10).*

"*But of Him are ye in Christ Jesus, who of God is made unto us wisdom, and righteousness, and sanctification, and redemption: that, according as it is written, He that glorieth, let him glory in the Lord*" *(I Cor. 1:30,31).*

When we are saved we are then dead and our lives are hid with Christ in God (Col. 3:3). When we are saved we "sit together in heavenly places in Christ Jesus" (Eph. 2:6). When we are saved we are sealed by the Holy Spirit until the day of redemption (Eph. 4:30). When we are saved we are covered by the blood, sealed by the Spirit, *complete in Christ* who is our wisdom, our righteousness, our sancti-

127

fication, and our redemption. God would cease to be GOD if He should lay anything to the charge of the believer.

2. *"Who shall lay anything to the charge of God's elect?"*
CAN CHRIST?

Let the Word answer: "While we were yet sinners, *Christ died* for us!" (Rom. 5:8). Jesus was *in the beginning* with the Father, He was *one* with the Father, He shared the *glory* of the Father. But He left that glory, He left the bosom of the Father, and came to this earth to make known the love of God to man (John 1:14,18). Jesus Himself said, "Therefore doth my Father love me, because I LAY DOWN MY LIFE, that I might take it again. No man taketh it from me, but I lay it down of myself. I have power to lay it down, and I have power to take it again. This commandment have I received of my Father. . . My sheep hear my voice, and I know them, and they follow me: And I give unto them eternal life; and they shall never perish, neither shall any man pluck them out of my hand. My Father, which gave them me, is greater than all; and no man is able to pluck them out of my Father's hand. I AND MY FATHER ARE ONE" (John 10:17–30).

In Luke 19:10 He said, ". . . the Son of man is come to seek and to save that which was lost." His invitation was, "Come unto me, *ALL* . . . he that cometh unto me I will in no wise cast out!" When we believe in the finished work and the shed blood of Jesus, He comes into our heart, He is in us and we are in Him. We are His children, He is our Saviour, and He sits at the right hand of God the Father making intercession for us:

"For there is one God, and one Mediator between God and men, the Man Christ Jesus" (I Tim. 2:5).

"God, who at sundry times and in divers manners

spake in time past unto the fathers by the prophets, hath in these last days spoken unto us by His Son, whom He hath appointed heir of all things, by whom also He made the worlds; who being the brightness of His glory, and the express image of His person, and upholding all things by the word of His power, when He had by Himself purged our sins, sat down on the right hand of the Majesty on high" (Heb. 1:1–3).

The born again believer is a child of God, an heir of God and joint-heir with Jesus. Is it possible then to condemn him and consign him to the lake of fire? *Who can send him there*? "Who IS he that condemneth? IT IS CHRIST THAT DIED, yea rather, that is risen again, who is even at the right hand of God, who also maketh intercession for us" (Rom. 8:34). Jesus, the Saviour of the believer (the elect), died and rose again that we might be saved. He is seated at the right hand of God the Father to make intercession for us, and we are more than *conquerors* through Him. Since He now intercedes for us, *who SHALL separate us from the love of God*?

Dearly beloved, consider this: The born again believer is partaker of divine nature (II Pet. 1:4; Rom. 8:9, 14, 16; John 3:5; I Cor. 12:12,13; Col. 3:3; Eph. 4:30). Therefore if the believer is charged with sin and iniquity, then JESUS is also charged with sin and iniquity, because the believer is in Christ and Christ is in the believer. Since that be true, and since Christ died to save us and ever lives to intercede for us, since "we shall be saved by His life"(Rom. 5:10), then Christ will not, He cannot, lay anything to the charge of God's elect! We are His purchased possession, His redeemed children. It was He who MADE us God's elect, and He will KEEP us God's elect. We are more than conquerors and overcomers because greater is He who is in us than he who is in the world (I John 4:4).

3. *"Who shall lay anything to the charge of God's elect?"*
   CAN THE HOLY SPIRIT?

God the Father so loved us that He gave His only begotten Son to *die* for us. *Jesus* loved us so much that He *willingly* laid His life down that we might be saved through faith in His shed blood. But in John 6:44 Jesus said, "No man can come to me, except the Father which hath sent me draw him . . . ." The believer could not have *become* one of the elect had not the Holy Spirit convicted and drawn him to the Lord.

To His disciples Jesus said, "Nevertheless I tell you the truth: It is expedient for you that I go away: for if I go not away, the Comforter (the Holy Spirit) will not come unto you; but if I depart, I will send Him unto you. *And when He is come, He will reprove the world of sin, and of righteousness, and of judgment:* of sin, because they believe not on me; of righteousness, because I go to my Father, and ye see me no more; of judgment, because the prince of this world is judged" (John 16:7–11).

The Holy Spirit not only convicts us and draws us to God; He is also the attending Physician at the new birth – we are *born* of the Spirit: "Except a man be born of water *and of the Spirit*, he cannot enter into the kingdom of God" (John 3:5). The moment we are born into God's family, the Holy Spirit baptizes us into the body of Christ (the New Testament Church) (I Cor. 12:12,13; Eph. 5:25–30).

Not only does the Holy Spirit convict us, draw us, and "born" us; He also *leads* us (Rom. 8:14). He takes up His abode in our heart (Rom. 8:9), we *walk* in the Spirit and therefore we do not fulfill the lust of the flesh: "This I say then, Walk in the Spirit, and ye shall not fulfil the lust of the flesh" (Gal. 5:16). The Spirit leads us into the paths of righteousness, and as He leads us He testifies to us that we are sons of God (Rom. 8:16). And "if the Spirit of Him that raised up Jesus from the dead dwell in you, *He that raised up Christ from the dead shall also quicken YOUR mortal bodies* by His Spirit that dwelleth in you" (Rom. 8:11).

Therefore, the Holy Spirit cannot lay anything to the charge of God's elect because HE is the One who abides within us to lead us into paths of righteousness for the name's sake of God, even Jesus the Son.

4.   *"Who shall lay anything to the charge of God's elect?"*

   CAN SIN?

Romans 6:23 tells us that *"the wages of sin is death,"* and James 1:15 says, ". . . *sin, when it is finished, bringeth forth death!"* Sin and death are synonymous; the soul that sinneth shall *surely* die—but listen to these words that fell from the lips of the sinless Son of God:

"Verily, verily, I say unto you, *He that heareth my Word, and believeth on Him that sent me, hath everlasting life, and shall not come into condemnation; but is passed from death unto life"* (John 5:24).

Notice: Jesus did not say, "He that heareth my Word and believeth on Him that sent me MAY have eternal life, or *may* have eternal life *at the END of life's journey."* He spoke in the present tense—*"HATH everlasting life . . . IS passed from death unto life."* The believer possesses eternal life NOW — and life and death do not abide in the same heart.   "She that liveth in pleasure is dead while she liveth" (I Tim. 5:6).   The Holy Spirit abides in the bosom of every born again believer; therefore the believer is alive unto God, he has passed from death unto life NOW.

131

"And you hath He quickened, who were dead in trespasses and sins . . . Even when we were dead in sins, (God) hath quickened us together with Christ . . . and hath raised us up together, and made us sit together in heavenly places in Christ Jesus" (Eph. 2:1–6).

Can SIN lay anything to the charge of God's elect? Let God's Word answer: "For He (God) hath made Him (Jesus) to be sin for us, who knew no sin (Jesus was sinless); that we might be made *the righteousness of God* IN HIM" (II Cor. 5:21).

Dear believer, when one puts his trust in the shed blood of Jesus Christ, the spotless Lamb of God, and receives Him as personal Saviour, *that one is made the righteousness of God in Jesus.* In Christ we are righteous, holy, pure, and complete; therefore sin cannot condemn us, sin cannot lay anything to our charge. The sin-question is settled forever since Jesus took our sins, bore them in His own body, and nailed them to the cross.

5. *"Who shall lay anything to the charge of God's elect?"*

    CAN SATAN?

The devil is still operating in this world – sometimes as an angel of light, sometimes as a roaring lion; but he is a defeated foe. In the Garden of Eden God said to him, "I will put enmity between thee and the woman, and between thy seed and her seed; it shall bruise thy head, and thou shalt bruise his heel" (Gen. 3:15). Satan bruised the heel of Jesus on Calvary – the Lamb of God was *bruised for our iniquities*; but in the by-and-by Jesus will crush Satan's head and will personally put him into the lake of fire that burns with brimstone forever (Rev. 20:1–10).

John 19:30 tells us that just before Jesus literally gave His spirit back to the heavenly Father, "He said, IT

IS FINISHED! and He bowed His head, and gave up the ghost." *WHAT was finished*? What did Jesus come to earth TO finish? We find the answer in Hebrews 2:9, 14, 15:

"But we see Jesus, who was made a little lower than the angels for the suffering of death, crowned with glory and honour; that He by the grace of God should taste death for every man. . . Forasmuch then as the children are partakers of flesh and blood, He also Himself likewise took part of the same; that through death He might destroy him that had the power of death, that is, the devil; and deliver them who through fear of death were all their lifetime subject to bondage."

Jesus was made a little lower than the angels, He was given a body of flesh, for the specific purpose of dying. The wages of sin is death. Jesus came to pay the sin-debt, and in order to pay the sin-debt it was a divine imperative that one die — but that one must be perfect, holy, and sinless. Therefore Jesus was the only one who *could* pay the sin-debt. He took flesh that He might taste death for every man. He received His flesh from the Virgin Mary (Luke 1:26–28); He received His blood from God (Acts 20:28). In His flesh He died — but death could not hold Him. He defeated death, He defeated him who had the *power* of death — that is, the devil; and thus delivered them "who through *fear* of death were all their lifetime subject to bondage."

Thus Jesus finished the work the Father sent Him to do. He came into the world to taste death for every man and to destroy him who had the power of death. He was manifested to take away our sins, although IN HIM IS NO SIN. And since He conquered the world, the flesh, the devil, death, hell, and the grave, He completely defeated the program of Satan to damn the human race! Therefore Satan cannot condemn us, he cannot lay anything to the charge of

133

God's elect; he cannot separate the blood-washed believer from the love of God.

6. *"Who shall lay anything to the charge of God's elect?"*

CAN THE LAW?

There are those today who teach that we must keep the commandments in order to be saved. God anointed the Apostle Paul and sent him as minister to the Gentiles; and through him the Holy Ghost declared, "Therefore by the deeds of the law there shall no flesh be justified in His sight: for by the law is the knowledge of sin" (Rom. 3:20). This verse makes it very clear that the law was not given to save men. "By the law is the knowledge of SIN" – and the Bible definition of sin is *"transgression of God's Holy Law."* I John 3:4 tells us, "Whosoever committeth sin transgresseth also the law: for sin is the transgression of the law."

Has the law then been *annulled*? or did Jesus *destroy* the law? No. In Matthew 5:17,18 He said, "Think not that I am come to destroy the law, or the prophets: I am not come to destroy, but to fulfil. For verily I say unto you, Till heaven and earth pass, one jot or one tittle shall in no wise pass from the law, *till all be fulfilled."* Jesus fulfilled the law – and He filled it *full!* He satisfied every demand of God's righteousness and holiness, He completely satisfied the *justice* of God. Therefore, IN Jesus we are law-keepers – but ONLY in Jesus. No man except Jesus Christ has ever kept God's law perfectly.

In Romans 10:1–4 Paul said, "Brethren, my heart's desire and prayer to God for Israel is, that they might be saved. For I bear them record that they have a zeal of God, but not according to knowledge. For they being ignorant of God's righteousness, and going about to establish their own righteousness, have not submitted themselves unto the righteousness of God. *For CHRIST is the END of the law for righteousness to every one that believeth.*"

Christ fulfilled every jot and tittle of the law, He is the END of the law for righteousness to believers, and therefore the law cannot lay anything to the charge of God's elect. James 2:10 tells us that whosoever shall keep the whole law and yet offend in *even one point* is guilty of breaking *the entire law.* The individual who breaks the least of the commandments is guilty of breaking ALL of them; but when we believe on Jesus we keep the law perfectly IN HIM. And since the believer is in Christ, *the law cannot condemn.*

7. *"Who shall lay anything to the charge of God's elect?"* CAN DEATH?

Writing to the believers in Corinth Paul said, "The last enemy that shall be destroyed is death" (I Cor. 15:26). In II Corinthians 5:6 he said, "Therefore we are always confident, knowing that, whilst we are at home *in the body*, we are *absent* from the Lord."

Death has no sting for the believer: "So when this corruptible shall have put on incorruption, and this mortal shall have put on immortality, then shall be brought to pass the saying that is written, *Death is swallowed up in victory.* O death, where is thy sting? O grave, where is thy victory? The sting of death is sin; and the strength of sin is the law. But thanks be to God, which giveth us the victory through our Lord Jesus Christ" (I Cor. 15:54–57).

According to I Corinthians 15:51, 52 there will be saints living when Jesus comes—saints who will be changed "in a moment, in the twinkling of an eye," from mortality to immortality; but if Jesus delays His coming, you and I

135

have an appointment with death. Yet for the believer *death has no sting*, death holds no *fear* (Heb. 2:14,15).

Jesus tasted death for every man (Heb. 2:9). He removed the sting of death for the Christian (I Cor. 15:55). He possesses the *keys* of death (Rev. 1:18). Therefore death is a defeated foe. O yes, death still operates in this world, but it has no claim on the believer. The split second a Christian departs this life, the spirit goes to be with the Lord Jesus Christ. Paul believed and preached this (II Cor. 5:6; Phil. 1:21–24). The believer does not *desire* to die; we love life, we love to win souls, witness for Jesus, and fellowship with our friends and families; but we do not *fear* death because it has no claim on us. Death cannot lay anything to the charge of God's elect.

Is This Fatalism?

Some who read this message will immediately declare that I believe in fatalism. Others will declare me to be a false prophet. In either instance I plead "Not guilty!" In the tremendous eighth chapter of Romans from which the Scripture for our text was taken, we read in the opening verse: "There is therefore now no condemnation to them which are in Christ Jesus, who walk not after the flesh, but after the Spirit."

Here we have a divine fact stated in words that are easy to understand. *Right now*, this very second, there is *no condemnation* to them which are in Christ Jesus; there is no condemnation to the born again, blood-washed believer. Notice the verse does not say "there is therefore now no condemnation to *church members*, or to those who merely *profess religion*." It makes it very plain that there is no condemnation "*to them which are IN CHRIST JESUS.*" The person who is in Christ Jesus is truly born again, truly washed in the blood, truly saved eternally by God's grace.

Now notice the last part of the verse: ". . . who walk not after the FLESH, but after the SPIRIT." It does not say, "IF we walk not after the flesh." The statement is clear, concise, understandable. It says, "who WALK NOT after the flesh." Those who are IN CHRIST JESUS do *not* walk after the flesh, but after the Spirit. We follow the Spirit because He abides in us to lead us, and Romans 8:14 plainly tells us that as many as are led by the Spirit of God are the sons of God. Friend, if you *live* in the flesh and *walk* after the flesh, then according to God's Word you are not a Christian.

So much of the misunderstanding and division among believers comes about as a result of misunderstanding concerning what it means to BE a Christian. Not everyone is a Christian who *professes* to be one. Not every church member is a truly born again believer. Only those who are IN CHRIST are Christians – born again, redeemed by the blood. These make up "the elect."

We read further in this same chapter of Romans, "And we know that ALL THINGS work together for good to them that love God, to them who are the called according to His purpose" (v. 28). Believers do not "think," or "hope," or "guess." We KNOW that all things work together for our good. Notice the Holy Spirit does not say that each and every little *individual* thing that happens to a believer is for his good, but rather that *"all things work TOGETHER for good."* From the moment one is born again until the split second he departs this life to be with the Lord, *whatever happens to that person is for his good and to the glory of God.*

WHY? The answer is in the next verse: *"For whom He did foreknow, He also did predestinate to be conformed*

137

to the image of His Son, that He might be the firstborn among many brethren." Every born again, blood-washed, redeemed child of God is predestined to be conformed to the image of God's own dear Son; and thus, whatever happens to the true believer, it is only part of God's molding, shaping, and making that believer into the image of the Lord Jesus Christ.

Beloved, try to realize that God the Father is a million times more interested than YOU are in the way you live and what you accomplish as a Christian. He wants His children to bring glory and honor to the name of Jesus. He *saves* us for Christ's sake (Eph. 4:32), we are witnesses, we are living epistles read of men (II Cor. 3:2), we display *Christ* as we travel through this life, and God has more concern than WE do about what we do and how we live as Christians. He purchased our salvation, He has provided power that we may be victorious, and when we refuse to walk as He would have us walk He chastens us. But whatever comes our way, we have God's promise that "all things work *together*" for our good and His eternal glory.

This promise is not to just a select, elect little group, but to ALL who love God and are called according to His purpose. Therefore we can ask with spiritual boldness, *"Who SHALL lay anything to the charge of God's elect?"* Since God is God He is holy, just, and righteous. Can HE condemn us? Would He WANT to condemn us? *"It is God that justifieth."* God loved us so much that He gave His only begotten Son and allowed Him to taste death for us, allowed Him to bear our sins in His own body on the cross in order to redeem us. The same God has provided victory, grace, and strength to travel life's journey. It is God who predestinated us to be conformed to the image of His Son. Since God is God, He cannot and He will not lay anything

138

to the charge of His born again ones.

Would *Christ* lay anything to the charge of one whom He has saved? Would He condemn one who has trusted in His shed blood and finished work? No. It was Christ who loved us enough to die for us and who even now sits at the right hand of the Father to *intercede* for us. Christ lives—not to condemn us, but to stand in our place before God the heavenly Father.

Can *the Holy Spirit* lay anything to the charge of God's elect? No. It is the Spirit who leads us into paths of right living. He abides within our heart to direct us, to assure us, to lead us around the pitfalls of Satan. It is the third Person of the Trinity who *seals* us until that day of redemption; and although it is possible for the believer to *grieve* the Spirit, He would not accuse or condemn us.

Can *sin* condemn us? No—the spotless Son of God was made to be sin for us, and we are justified through His shed blood. When we are in Him, truly born again, we are just as just as Jesus is just; and when God looks upon us He does not see our sin: He sees the precious blood of Jesus that covers the believer (II Cor. 5:21; Eph. 1:6,7).

Can *Satan* condemn us? No—although he would *like* to! He *accuses* the brethren (Rev. 12:10), but he cannot condemn us. He is a conquered foe and he knows it. Jesus stood face to face with him and defeated him (Matt. 4:1–11). He overcame the world, the flesh, the devil, death, hell, and the grave; therefore *Satan cannot* lay anything to the charge of God's elect.

Can *the law* condemn us? No; because Jesus fulfilled every jot and tittle of the law and we stand IN HIM before God as perfect law-keepers!

Can *death* condemn us when we come to the end of

139

life's journey? No. Jesus took a body, and IN that body He tasted death for every man. He removed the sting of death for the Christian. He died — but it was not possible that death should hold Him. He rose again — and because HE lives, WE live.

There is NO ONE in heaven, in earth, or under the earth who can lay *anything* to the charge of God's elect!

Are You A Believer?

"Wherefore the rather, brethren, give diligence to make your calling and election sure: for if ye do these things, ye shall never fall" (II Pet. 1:10).

You may be a church member, you may have "religion," but *are you a born again believer*? Stop now and ask yourself, "Did I simply join a church? Did I just receive baptism? Or have I *truly been born again*?" In John 3:3 and 5 Jesus declared to Nicodemus that no person can enter the kingdom of heaven *without* being born again. In Luke 13:3 and 5 He declared, "Except ye repent, ye shall all likewise perish!" Have *you* repented? Have *you* been born again? Can you remember a time, a place (not necessarily a date or an hour, but *an experience*) when you truly repented of your sins and received Jesus as your Saviour? If you cannot remember such an experience, bow upon your knees this moment and put your faith in the shed blood and the finished work of the Lamb of God!

Here is the key to heaven: *". . . If thou shalt confess with thy mouth the Lord Jesus, and shalt believe in thine heart that God hath raised Him from the dead, thou shalt be saved. For with the heart man believeth unto righteousness; and with the mouth confession is made unto salvation"* (Rom. 10:9,10).

Have YOU done this? Have you confessed with your

140

mouth that Jesus is Christ, the Son of God? and that He died on the cross, was buried, and the third day rose again? Do you believe that He now lives to make intercession for all who will believe on Him? If you have not believed in your heart and confessed with your mouth, do it now!

The jailer at Philippi asked Paul and Silas, "Sirs, what must I do to be saved?" They replied, "Believe on the Lord Jesus Christ, and thou shalt be saved, and thy house. And they spake unto him the Word of the Lord, and to all that were in his house" (Acts 16:30-32).

Jesus said, "Verily, verily, I say unto you, He that heareth my word, and believeth on Him that sent me, hath everlasting life, and shall not come into condemnation; but is passed from death unto life" (John 5:24).

Hear the Word of God, believe the Word of God, receive Jesus on the terms of the Gospel, "and thou shalt be saved."

"For by grace are ye saved through faith; and that not of yourselves: it is the gift of God: not of works, lest any man should boast" (Eph. 2:8,9).

We are saved by God's grace. Faith in the finished work of Jesus brings saving grace to the heart. Believe on the Lord Jesus Christ this moment, receive Him by faith. Then bow your head and thank Him for saving your soul!

Now That You Are A Believer

You are one of the "elect." You are hid with Christ in God, you possess the Holy Spirit, and you are sealed until the day of redemption. You are an overcomer, and now YOU can ask, "Who shall lay anything to the charge of God's elect? . . . Who shall separate us from the love of Christ? Shall tribulation, or distress, or persecution, or famine, or nakedness, or peril, or sword? . . . Nay, in all

141

these things we are more than conquerors through Him that loved us. *For I am persuaded, that neither death, nor life, nor angels, nor principalities, nor powers, nor things present, nor things to come, nor height, nor depth, NOR ANY OTHER CREATURE, shall be able to separate us from the love of God, which is in Christ Jesus our Lord!*" (Rom. 8:33–39).

WHY HAS GOD BEEN SILENT?

WHY HAS GOD BEEN SILENT?

The question is often asked, "Why has God been silent since Jesus went back to heaven, nineteen hundred years ago?" The answer is found in II Timothy 3:16,17:

"All Scripture is given by inspiration of God, and is profitable for doctrine, for reproof, for correction, for instruction in righteousness: that the man of God may be perfect, throughly furnished unto all good works."

I believe the Bible is the Word of God, I believe every word IN the Bible is the Word of God, and I believe the Bible is *all there IS* of the Word of God. I do not believe that there are any other sacred writings. Our Bible is composed of sixty-six books written by some forty different persons in all stations of life. The writing of those sixty-six books covered a period of approximately 1600 years—from about 1500 B. C. when Moses wrote the first five books in our Bible (under the inspiration of Almighty God and sound of the thunders of Sinai) up to about A. D. 97 when God gave John the Beloved (a "son of thunder"—Mark 3:17) the glorious book of The Revelation. Although many years and many miles separated the writers, the Bible is in perfect harmony from Genesis 1:1 through Revelation 22:21.

There is a reason why God has been silent for more than nineteen centuries, and that reason will be the subject of this message.

I

God revealed to *Adam* that He would send the Saviour. Adam was the first man on this earth. God created him from the dust of the ground, breathed into his nostrils the breath of life, and he became a living soul (Gen. 2:7). He then removed a rib from Adam's side, and from that rib He created Eve and gave her to Adam to be his wife (Gen. 2:21,22). In Genesis 3:15 God promised the Saviour who would crush Satan's head. He was to be "*the seed of the woman*," not the seed of the *man*.

God has a program, a plan, and He follows that plan. He is not in a hurry, His ways are not our ways, His thoughts are not our thoughts. He is sovereign — He knows the end in the beginning, He knows all that lies *between* the beginning and the end. Therefore, at the appointed time in His program He did exactly what He promised Adam He would do:

"But when the fulness of the time was come, God sent forth His Son, *made of a WOMAN*, made under the law, to redeem them that were under the law, that we might receive the adoption of sons" (Gal. 4:4,5).

We read the story in Luke 1:26–35: "And in the sixth month the angel Gabriel was sent from God unto a city of Galilee, named Nazareth, to a virgin espoused to a man whose name was Joseph, of the house of David; and the virgin's name was Mary. And the angel came in unto her, and said, Hail, thou that art highly favoured, the Lord is is with thee: blessed art thou among women. And when she saw him, she was troubled at his saying, and cast in her mind what manner of salutation this should be.

"And the angel said unto her, Fear not, Mary: for thou hast found favour with God. And, behold, thou shalt conceive in thy womb, and bring forth a Son, and shalt call His name JESUS. He shall be great, and shall be called the Son of the Highest: and the Lord God shall give unto Him the throne of His father David: and He shall reign over the house of Jacob for ever; and of His kingdom there shall be no end.

"Then said Mary unto the angel, How shall this be, seeing I know not a man? And the angel answered and said unto her, The Holy Ghost shall come upon thee, and the power of the Highest shall overshadow thee: therefore also that holy thing which shall be born of thee shall be called the Son of God."

More than four thousand years before this, God had revealed to Adam that the Saviour would be the seed of *woman*, and in Matthew 1:18–25 we read, "Now the birth of Jesus Christ was on this wise: When as His mother Mary was espoused to Joseph, before they came together, she was found with child of the Holy Ghost. Then Joseph her husband, being a just man, and not willing to make her a publick example, was minded to put her away privily.

"But while he thought on these things, behold, the angel of the Lord appeared unto him in a dream, saying, Joseph, thou son of David, fear not to take unto thee Mary thy wife: for that which is conceived in her is of the Holy Ghost. And she shall bring forth a Son, and thou shalt call His name JESUS: for He shall save His people from their sins.

"Now all this was done, that it might be fulfilled which was spoken of the Lord by the prophet, saying, Behold, a virgin shall be with child, and shall bring forth a Son, and they shall call His name Emmanuel, which being interpreted is, God with us.

"Then Joseph being raised from sleep did as the angel of the Lord had bidden him, and took unto him his wife: and knew her not till she had brought forth her firstborn Son: and he called His name JESUS."

Liberals and modernists deny the virgin birth. Many

learned men declare that it would be a scientific impossibility for a *virgin* to give birth to a child; but I am happy to declare that "scientific impossibilities" are God's opportunities to show man that God is God and there is *nothing* impossible with HIM! Mary DID conceive, and she brought forth a Son — not the son of Joseph, but the Son of GOD.

II

To *Abraham* God revealed the nation out of which the Saviour would come and with which He would be identified:

"Now the Lord had said unto Abram, Get thee out of thy country, and from thy kindred, and from thy father's house, unto a land that I will shew thee: and I will make of thee a great nation, and I will bless thee, and make thy name great; and thou shalt be a blessing: And I will bless them that bless thee, and curse him that curseth thee: and in thee shall all families of the earth be blessed" (Gen. 12:1–3).

Notice the tremendous truths set forth in these three short verses. God spoke to Abraham and commanded him to leave his country, his kinfolk, and his father's house, and travel "unto a land that I will shew thee." He did not tell Abraham where he was going; He simply said, "I will *shew* thee." Then notice the promises God gave him:

"I will make of thee a great nation.

I will bless thee, and make thy name great,

and thou shalt be a blessing.

I will bless them that bless thee

and curse him that curseth thee,

AND IN THEE SHALL ALL FAMILIES OF THE EARTH BE BLESSED."

This last promise points to the Messiah, for it was through the line of Abraham that the Messiah would come.

More than two thousand years later, the Holy Ghost made this tremendous truth known to us, through the inspired pen of the Apostle Paul:

"Christ hath redeemed us from the curse of the law, being made a curse for us: for it is written, Cursed is every one that hangeth on a tree: *That the blessing of Abraham might come on the Gentiles through Jesus Christ; that we might receive the promise of the Spirit through faith.* Brethren, I speak after the manner of men; Though it be but a *man's* covenant, yet if it be confirmed, no man disannulleth, or addeth thereto. *Now to Abraham and his seed were the promises made. He saith not, And to seeds, as of many: but as of one, And to thy seed, which is Christ*" (Gal. 3:13—16).

The R. S. V. translation butchers verse 3 of the passage from Genesis 12. In the R. S. V. Bible this verse reads, "I will bless those who bless you, and him who curses you I will curse; *and by you all families of the earth WILL BLESS THEMSELVES.*" But the families of the earth cannot bless *themselves.* Abraham could not bless *himself.* God gave him a command, he obeyed, and when he *obeyed* God, God blessed him. He gave him a great name, made him a great man, he became "the father of the faithful," and through his seed and his nation the Messiah, Saviour of the world, was born.

Please notice the first phrase of Genesis 12:4: "SO ABRAM DEPARTED, AS THE LORD HAD SPOKEN UNTO HIM." Abraham did not demand further instructions or explanations; he did not ask for more knowledge of *where* he was going, *why* he was going, or *what he would find* when he arrived there. Beloved, if we hope to do business

149

with God, if we hope to be what He wants us to be, if we want Him to smile upon us in our Christian living and stewardship, then we must let Him do the instructing while we listen, obey, and move as He orders. We may not understand where, why, or what the outcome will be; but if God orders it, we can rest assured that *whatever* it is, it will come out all right.

III

To *Jacob* God revealed that the Messiah would be of the tribe of Judah:

"The sceptre shall not depart from Judah, nor a lawgiver from between his feet, *until Shiloh come*; and unto Him shall the gathering of the people be" (Gen. 49:10).

"Shiloh" is but one of the many names of our wonderful Saviour. Isaiah tells us that "His name shall be called Wonderful, Counsellor, The mighty God, The everlasting Father, The Prince of Peace" (Isa. 9:6). In various places throughout the Bible we read where His name is "The Vine . . . the Door . . . the Bread . . . the Alpha, the Omega . . . the Rose of Sharon . . . the Lily of the Valley . . . the Bright and Morning Star," and many others. God is simply telling His people that the Saviour would come through the tribe of Judah – and the Jews as we know them today are descendants of Judah. To the Samaritan woman at the well Jesus said, "Salvation is of the Jews" (John 4:22).

The nation of Israel—including the tribe of Judah— grievously backslid and departed from the Lord, but God always spared a faithful remnant. Many times Satan *almost wiped out* the seed through which the Lord Jesus would be born, but he could never succeed in completely stamping out the line through which Jesus was to come. All hell with all of its demon power could not stop the coming of

150

the Messiah, the Lord Jesus Christ.

IV

To *David* God revealed that the promised Seed would be a member of his family:

". . . Also the Lord telleth thee that He will make thee an house. And when thy days be fulfilled, and thou shalt sleep with thy fathers, I will set up thy seed after thee, which shall proceed out of thy bowels, and I will establish His kingdom. He shall build an house for my name, and I will establish the throne of His kingdom for ever" (II Sam. 7:11–13).

God revealed to David that although *he himself* would depart this life and sleep with his fathers, *his seed* would not cease to be. When Gabriel revealed to Mary that she was to be the mother of God's Son, he said, "He shall be great, and shall be called the Son of the Highest: *and the Lord God shall give unto Him the throne of His father David: AND HE SHALL REIGN OVER THE HOUSE OF JACOB FOR EVER; AND OF HIS KINGDOM THERE SHALL BE NO END*" (Luke 1:32,33).

Through the pen of Luke the Holy Spirit has recorded the fulfillment of the prophecy of centuries before as recorded in II Samuel 7. Mary *did* conceive, she *did* bring forth a Son, He was great, He was called the Son of God— and one day the Lord God Almighty *will* give to Him the throne of David. Yes, the throne of David is a historical fact just as truly as the throne of the Caesars is a historical fact; and one day Jesus will sit on a literal throne in the city of Jerusalem and will reign over the house of Jacob as prophesied.

In Acts 15:13–18 we read, "And after they had held their peace, James answered, saying, Men and brethren, hearken unto me: Simeon hath declared how God at the first did visit the Gentiles, to take out of them a people for His name. And to this agree the words of the prophets; as it is written, After this I will return, and will build again the tabernacle of David, which is fallen down; and I will build again the ruins thereof, and I will set it up: That the residue of men might seek after the Lord, and all the Gentiles, upon whom my name is called, saith the Lord, who doeth all these things. Known unto God are all His works from the beginning of the world."

When we look around us today we might think that Satan has everything going his way; believers appear to be in the minority and we seem to be losing the battle — but not so! One day Jesus will come and will put down the ungodly rule that controls this world today. The knowledge of the Lord will then cover the earth as the waters cover the sea. Men *will* beat their swords into plowshares and their spears into pruning hooks. There *will* be peace on earth, good will toward men; Jesus *will* sit on the throne of His father David in Jerusalem and will reign for one thousand glorious years right here upon this earth — and WE (the born again ones, the bride of Christ) will reign with Him. *That* will be the grand and glorious Millennium promised to the seed of Abraham:

"And I saw thrones, and they sat upon them, and judgment was given unto them: and I saw the souls of them that were beheaded for the witness of Jesus, and for the Word of God, and which had not worshipped the beast, neither his image, neither had received his mark upon their foreheads, or in their hands; and they lived and reigned with Christ a thousand years. But the rest of the dead lived not again until the thousand years were finished. This is the first resurrection. *Blessed and holy is*

152

he that hath part in the first resurrection: on such the second death hath no power, BUT THEY SHALL BE PRIESTS OF GOD AND OF CHRIST, AND SHALL REIGN WITH HIM A THOUSAND YEARS" (Rev. 20:4–6).

V

To *Daniel* God revealed *the time* when Jesus the Messiah would appear:

"Seventy weeks are determined upon thy people and upon thy holy city, to finish the transgression, and to make an end of sins, and to make reconciliation for iniquity, and to bring in everlasting righteousness, and to seal up the vision and prophecy, and to anoint the most Holy. Know therefore and understand, that from the going forth of the commandment to restore and to build Jerusalem unto the Messiah the Prince shall be seven weeks, and threescore and two weeks: the street shall be built again, and the wall, even in troublous times" (Dan. 9:24,25).

The weeks spoken of in verse 24 are *sevens of years*— not seven days; each week represents a seven-year period— seventy weeks of seven years each. It was revealed to Daniel that *within* these weeks the national chastisement of Israel must be ended and the nation re-established in its own land in everlasting righteousness.

These seventy weeks are divided into three groups: *Seven* weeks (49 years); *sixty-two* weeks (434 years); and *one* week of seven years (Dan. 9:25–27). In the first group of weeks (the first 49 years) the Holy City Jerusalem was to be rebuilt, and this was to be done in troublesome times. We find the record of this in the books of Ezra and Nehemiah, the period of forty-nine years *literally fulfilled as recorded.*

The second group of weeks (434 years) thereafter, the

Messiah was to come (verse 25). *This was fulfilled in the birth and manifestation of the Lord Jesus Christ.* Anyone who will take the time to study the books of Ezra, Nehemiah, and other prophecies concerning Israel and the rebuilding of Jerusalem can easily figure out these years exactly. The first forty-nine year period was literally fulfilled; the next period (434 years, or up to the birth of Messiah) was literally fulfilled; then in verse 26 we read: "And after threescore and two weeks *shall Messiah be cut off, but not for Himself*: and the people of the prince that shall come shall destroy the city and the sanctuary; and the end thereof shall be with a flood, and unto the end of the war desolations are determined."

This verse represents an indeterminate period — no definite number of years is fixed. The date of the crucifixion of the Christ is not fixed. It is only said that He will be "cut off" AFTER the threescore and two weeks. The second thing mentioned in verse 26 (the destruction of the Holy City Jerusalem) was literally fulfilled in A. D. 70. *"Unto the end"* does not give us a fixed number of years — that period has already lasted almost *two thousand* years. The Holy Spirit revealed to Daniel that there would be wars and desolations "unto the end," and if we study Matthew 24 we will find spelled out the things that *will* occur before the end of the age. It has been said that "the Old Testament is the New Testament *infolded*, and the New Testament is the Old Testament *unfolded*." The New Testament reveals to us that which was hidden from the prophets in the Old Testament era. Study carefully Matthew 13:11–17 and Ephesians 3:1–10.

In these Scriptures is revealed the fact that during this non-fixed period (which has already lasted almost 2,000 years) the mysteries of the kingdom of heaven would

154

be made known. Also during this time a people would be called out for His name, and then before the great and terrible day of tribulation the Church will be caught out, caught up to meet Jesus in the air. Study Matthew 13:1–50; 16:18; Romans 11:25; and I Thessalonians 4:13–18.

When the *seventieth* week will begin (to run a course of approximately 7 years), no one knows. The time of the climaxing of the Church Age is not revealed; but since it is a historical fact that the first two groups of years were literally fulfilled, we know the *last* period of years WILL be fulfilled. This will be the Great Tribulation period, yet future; but it *will* come to pass just as surely as the first two groups of years came to pass; and according to Matthew 24:22, "Except those days should be shortened, there should no flesh be saved: but for the elect's (Israel's) sake those days shall be shortened."

VI

To *Micah* God revealed *the town* in which the Messiah would be born:

"Now gather thyself in troops, O daughter of troops: he hath laid siege against us: they shall smite the judge of Israel with a rod upon the cheek. *BUT THOU, BETH-LEHEM EPHRATAH, THOUGH THOU BE LITTLE AMONG THE THOUSANDS OF JUDAH, yet OUT OF THEE SHALL HE COME FORTH UNTO ME that is to be ruler in Israel; whose goings forth have been from of old, from everlasting"* (Micah 5:1,2).

Seven hundred years after the Holy Ghost dictated these words to Micah, God spoke to Matthew and he wrote:

"*Now when Jesus was born IN BETHLEHEM OF JUDAEA* in the days of Herod the king, behold, there came wise men from the east to Jerusalem, saying, Where is He

155

that is born King of the Jews? for we have seen His star in the east, and are come to worship Him" (Matt. 2:1,2).

When King Herod heard about these things, he was troubled lest a king *should* be born, and he called together the chief priests and scribes and "demanded of them where Christ should be born." They replied, "IN BETHLEHEM OF JUDAEA, for thus it is written by the prophet." Herod then called the *wise men*, questioned them as to what time the star appeared, and sent them to Bethlehem to search for the child. He said, "Go and search diligently for the young child; and when ye have found Him, bring me word again, that I may come and worship Him also" (Matt. 2:8).

God *warned* the wise men, revealing to them that Herod did not want to worship the child, but rather to destroy Him, "and being warned of God in a dream that they should not return to Herod, they departed into their own country another way" (Matt. 2:12). The angel of the Lord then appeared to Joseph and warned him that he should take Jesus and His mother and flee into Egypt and remain there until God should send him word that Herod was dead. So Joseph "took the young child and His mother by night, and departed into Egypt."

"Then Herod, when he saw that he was mocked of the wise men, was exceeding wroth, and sent forth, and slew all the children that were in *Bethlehem*, and in all the coasts thereof, from two years old and under, according to the time which he had diligently enquired of the wise men" (Matt. 2:16).

The specific location of the birth of Jesus—Messiah, King, and Saviour—was prophesied seven centuries before He was born; and in the fulness of time God sent His Son,

born exactly AS prophesied, exactly WHERE prophesied—
in the little city of Bethlehem.

VII

To *Malachi* and to *Isaiah* God revealed that the Messiah would be preceded by a *forerunner*. Four centuries before the Lord Jesus was born in Bethlehem of Judaea, God spoke to Malachi and told him to write:

"Behold, I will send my messenger, and he shall prepare the way before me: and the Lord, whom ye seek, shall suddenly come to His temple, even the messenger of the covenant, whom ye delight in: behold, He shall come, saith the Lord of hosts. But who may abide the day of His coming? and who shall stand when He appeareth? for He is like a refiner's fire, and like fullers' soap: And He shall sit as a refiner and purifier of silver: and He shall purify the sons of Levi, and purge them as gold and silver, that they may offer unto the Lord an offering in righteousness. Then shall the offering of Judah and Jerusalem be pleasant unto the Lord, as in the days of old, and as in former years. And I will come near to you to judgment; and I will be a swift witness against the sorcerers, and against the adulterers, and against false swearers, and against those that oppress the hireling in his wages, the widow, and the fatherless, and that turn aside the stranger from his right, and fear not me, saith the Lord of hosts. For I am the Lord, I change not; therefore ye sons of Jacob are not consumed" (Mal. 3:1—6).

Four hundred years after God revealed to Malachi that there would be a forerunner to announce the coming of Messiah, God spoke to Matthew, and he penned down these inspired words:

"In those days came John the Baptist, preaching in the wilderness of Judaea, and saying, Repent ye: for the kingdom of heaven is at hand. For this is he that was spoken of by the prophet Esaias (Isa. 40:3), saying, The voice of one crying in the wilderness, Prepare ye the way of the Lord, make His paths straight.

"And the same John had his raiment of camel's hair, and a leathern girdle about his loins; and his meat was locusts and wild honey. Then went out to him Jerusalem, and all Judaea, and all the region round about Jordan, and were baptized of him in Jordan, confessing their sins.

"But when he saw many of the Pharisees and Sadducees come to his baptism, he said unto them, O generation of vipers, who hath warned you to flee from the wrath to come? Bring forth therefore fruits meet for repentance: And think not to say within yourselves, We have Abraham to our father: for I say unto you, that God is able of these stones to raise up children unto Abraham. And now also the axe is laid unto the root of the trees: therefore every tree which bringeth not forth good fruit is hewn down, and cast into the fire. I indeed baptize you with water unto repentance: but He that cometh after me is mightier than I, whose shoes I am not worthy to bear: He shall baptize you with the Holy Ghost, and with fire: Whose fan is in His hand, and He will throughly purge His floor, and gather His wheat into the garner; but He will burn up the chaff with unquenchable fire.

"Then cometh Jesus from Galilee to Jordan unto John, to be baptized of him. But John forbad Him, saying, I have need to be baptized of thee, and comest thou to me? And Jesus answering said unto him, Suffer it to be so now: for thus it becometh us to fulfil all righteousness. Then he suffered Him. And Jesus, when He was baptized, went up straightway out of the water: and, lo, the heavens were opened unto Him, and He saw the Spirit of God descending like a dove, and lighting upon Him: and lo a voice from heaven, saying, This is my beloved Son, in whom I am well pleased" (Matt. 3:1–17).

There was absolutely no excuse for the Jews' missing their Messiah. They had the Old Testament, and they had studied the books of Isaiah, Malachi, and others. They should have recognized John the Baptist, and if they had recognized him they certainly would have known the Messiah whom John announced. But they were blinded by "the god of this age," they did not recognize their Messiah, and they refused to receive Him. When Pilate asked, "Whom shall I release unto you?" they shouted, "Barabbas! Release Barabbas! Crucify Jesus! Let His blood be upon us and upon our children."

When we read the Old Testament, and as we study the New, we marvel that the Jews failed to recognize their Messiah and King, and that they rejected and crucified Him; but when we look around us, we marvel even more! What excuse have WE? We have the open Bible, the entire Word of God—*complete*. We have churches by the tens of thousands. We have Gospel tracts and *portions* of the Scriptures printed and distributed by the multi-millions. Yet the masses of the peoples of the world—including Americans—completely ignore the Saviour; they refuse to receive Him, they refuse to love Him and live for Him. They, too, choose to follow "the god of this age"—the devil.

VIII

To *Zechariah* God revealed that the Lord Jesus Christ would be *betrayed* and sold for the price of a slave—thirty pieces of silver:

"And I will feed the flock of slaughter, even you, O poor of the flock. And I took unto me two staves; the one I called Beauty, and the other I called Bands; and I fed the flock. Three shepherds also I cut off in one month; and my soul lothed them, and their soul also abhorred me.

"Then said I, I will not feed you: that that dieth, let it die; and that that is to be cut off, let it be cut off; and let the rest eat every one the flesh of another. And I took my staff, even Beauty, and cut it asunder, that I might break my covenant which I had made with all the people. And it was broken in that day: and so the poor of the flock

159

that waited upon me knew that it was the word of the Lord.

"AND I SAID UNTO THEM, IF YE THINK GOOD, GIVE ME MY PRICE; AND IF NOT, FORBEAR. SO THEY WEIGHED FOR MY PRICE THIRTY PIECES OF SILVER. And the Lord said unto me, Cast it unto the potter: a goodly price that I was prised at of them. And I took the thirty pieces of silver, and cast them to the potter in the house of the Lord. Then I cut asunder mine other staff, even Bands, that I might break the brotherhood between Judah and Israel" (Zech. 11:7—14).

These words were dictated to Zechariah by the Holy Ghost five centuries before Judas Iscariot walked into the office of the chief priests and did exactly what Zechariah had prophesied:

"Then one of the twelve, called Judas Iscariot, went unto the chief priests, and said unto them, What will ye give me, and I will deliver Him unto you? And they covenanted with him *for thirty pieces of silver.* And from that time he sought opportunity to betray Him.

"Now the first day of the feast of unleavened bread the disciples came to Jesus, saying unto Him, Where wilt thou that we prepare for thee to eat the passover? And He said, Go into the city to such a man, and say unto him, The Master saith, My time is at hand; I will keep the passover at thy house with my disciples. And the disciples did as Jesus had appointed them; and they made ready the passover.

"Now when the even was come, He sat down with the twelve. And as they did eat, He said, Verily I say unto you, that one of you shall betray me. And they were exceeding sorrowful, and began every one of them to say unto Him, Lord, is it I? And He answered and said, He that dippeth his hand with me in the dish, the same shall betray me. The Son of man goeth as it is written of Him: but woe unto that man by whom the Son of man is betrayed! it had been good for that man if he had not been born.

"Then Judas, which betrayed Him, answered and said, Master, is it I? He said unto him, Thou hast said" (Matt. 26:14—25).

160

In connection with this passage of Scripture, please study John 13:2—30.

In Luke's Gospel we read, "Now the feast of unleavened bread drew nigh, which is called the Passover. And the chief priests and scribes sought how they might kill Him; for they feared the people. Then entered Satan into Judas surnamed Iscariot, being of the number of the twelve. *And he went HIS WAY*, and communed with the chief priests and captains, how he might betray Him unto them. And they were glad, and covenanted to give him money. And he promised, and sought opportunity to betray Him unto them in the absence of the multitude" (Luke 22:1—6).

In these verses from Luke we find two of the saddest words in the Bible. Judas Iscariot had walked and talked with Jesus, had witnessed His mighty miracles, had been present when He taught. Yet after all that he had experienced in his association with the Lord Jesus, we read in this passage that he *"went HIS WAY"* — the way that led him to destruction and eternal damnation. *"His way"* was the way to personal fame — he followed Jesus for the glamor of it. He must have been an *unusual* person, for he was elected secretary and treasurer of the disciple band and he carried the money. *"His way"* was the way of greed and personal advancement. When Mary anointed the feet of Jesus with costly perfume, Judas protested. He said, "Why was not this ointment sold for three hundred pence, and given to the poor?" But he did not really care for the poor; he simply wanted more money in the bag so that he would have more to steal. (Read the account in John 12:1—6.) *"His way"* was the way of death: "There is a way which seemeth right unto a man, but the end thereof are the ways of death" (Prov. 14:12). The only RIGHT way is to walk with Jesus; He is the Way, the

Truth, and the Life. No man can come to the Father but by Him (John 14:6).

IX

To *Zechariah* God *also* revealed how the Messiah would ride into the Holy City, Jerusalem: "Rejoice greatly, O daughter of Zion; shout, O daughter of Jerusalem: behold, thy King cometh unto thee: He is just, and having salvation; lowly, and riding upon an ass, and upon a colt the foal of an ass" (Zech. 9:9).

Five centuries later the Holy Ghost spoke to Matthew and he penned these words:

"And when they drew nigh unto Jerusalem, and were come to Bethphage, unto the mount of Olives, then sent Jesus two disciples, saying unto them, Go into the village over against you, and straightway ye shall find an ass tied, and a colt with her: loose them, and bring them unto me. And if any man say ought unto you, ye shall say, The Lord hath need of them; and straightway he will send them.

"All this was done, that it might be fulfilled which was spoken by the prophet, saying, Tell ye the daughter of Sion, Behold, thy King cometh unto thee, meek, and sitting upon an ass, and a colt the foal of an ass.

"And the disciples went, and did as Jesus commanded them, and brought the ass, and the colt, and put on them their clothes, and they set Him thereon. And a very great multitude spread their garments in the way; others cut down branches from the trees, and strawed them in the way. And the multitudes that went before, and that followed, cried, saying, Hosanna to the son of David: Blessed is He that cometh in the name of the Lord; Hosanna in the highest. And when He was come into Jerusalem, all the city was moved, saying, Who is this? And the multitude said, This is Jesus the prophet of Nazareth of Galilee" (Matt. 21: 1–11).

The testimony of Matthew is sufficient—God does not need to say anything but once to make it so; but suppose

162

we let Luke also tell us of this event, the fulfillment of a prophecy five centuries after it was prophesied:

"And when He had thus spoken, He went before, ascending up to Jerusalem. And it came to pass, when He was come nigh to Bethphage and Bethany, at the mount called the mount of Olives, He sent two of His disciples, saying, Go ye into the village over against you; in the which at your entering ye shall find a colt tied, whereon yet never man sat: loose him, and bring him hither. And if any man ask you, Why do ye loose him? thus shall ye say unto him, Because the Lord hath need of him.

"And they that were sent went their way, and found even as He had said unto them. And as they were loosing the colt, the owners thereof said unto them, Why loose ye the colt? And they said, The Lord hath need of him. And they brought him to Jesus: and they cast their garments upon the colt, and they set Jesus thereon. And as He went, they spread their clothes in the way.

"And when He was come nigh, even now at the descent of the mount of Olives, the whole multitude of the disciples began to rejoice and praise God with a loud voice for all the mighty works that they had seen; saying, Blessed be the King that cometh in the name of the Lord: peace in heaven, and glory in the highest. And some of the Pharisees from among the multitude said unto Him, Master, rebuke thy disciples. And He answered and said unto them, I tell you that, if these should hold their peace, the stones would immediately cry out" (Luke 19:28—40).

X

To the *Psalmist* God revealed *the manner* of the death of Jesus:

"My God, my God, why hast thou forsaken me? Why art thou so far from helping me, and from the words of my roaring? O my God, I cry in the daytime, but thou hearest not; and in the night season, and am not silent. But thou art holy, O thou that inhabitest the praises of Israel. Our fathers trusted in thee: they trusted, and thou didst deliver them. They cried unto thee, and were delivered: they trusted in thee, and were not confounded.

"But I am a worm, and no man; a reproach of men, and despised of the people. *All they that see me laugh me to scorn: they shoot out the lip, they shake the head, saying, He trusted on the Lord that He would deliver Him: let Him deliver Him, seeing He delighted in Him.* But thou art He that took me out of the womb: thou didst make me hope when I was upon my mother's breasts. I was cast upon thee from the womb: thou art my God from my mother's belly. Be not far from me; for trouble is near; for there is none to help. Many bulls have compassed me: strong bulls of Bashan have beset me round. They gaped upon me with their mouths, as a ravening and a roaring lion. I am poured out like water, and all my bones are out of joint: my heart is like wax; it is melted in the midst of my bowels. My strength is dried up like a potsherd; and my tongue cleaveth to my jaws; and thou hast brought me into the dust of death.

"FOR DOGS HAVE COMPASSED ME: THE ASSEM-BLY OF THE WICKED HAVE INCLOSED ME: THEY PIERCED MY HANDS AND MY FEET. I MAY TELL ALL MY BONES: THEY LOOK AND STARE UPON ME. THEY PART MY GARMENTS AMONG THEM, AND CAST LOTS UPON MY VESTURE. But be not thou far from me, O Lord: O my strength, haste thee to help me. Deliver my soul from the sword; my darling from the power of the dog"* (Psalm 22:1—20).

To the Psalmist God also revealed that not one bone in the body of Jesus would be broken (Psalm 34:20).

From Psalm 16 we know that God revealed to David the fact that death could not hold the Christ:

"The Lord is the portion of mine inheritance and of my cup: thou maintainest my lot. The lines are fallen unto me in pleasant places; yea, I have a goodly heritage. I will bless the Lord, who hath given me counsel: my reins also instruct me in the night seasons. I have set the Lord always before me: because He is at my right hand, I shall not be moved. Therefore my heart is glad, and my glory rejoiceth: *MY FLESH ALSO SHALL REST IN HOPE. FOR THOU WILT NOT LEAVE MY SOUL IN HELL; NEITHER WILT THOU SUFFER THINE HOLY ONE TO SEE CORRUPTION.* Thou wilt shew me the path of life: in thy presence is fulness of joy; at thy right hand there are pleasures for evermore" (Psalm 16:5–11).

Centuries after these tremendous truths were revealed to David, God spoke to John the beloved disciple and HE penned down *the fulfillment* of those prophecies. Jesus was arrested in Gethsemane, Peter denied Him, He was brought before Pilate who examined and cross-examined Him, and three times confessed, "I find in Him no fault at all" (John 18:38; 19:4,6); but the Jews demanded that He be crucified. They said to Pilate, "If thou let this man go, thou art not Caesar's friend: whosoever maketh himself a king speaketh against Caesar" (John 19:12). So Pilate allowed them to take Jesus and crucify Him:

"And He bearing His cross went forth into a place called the place of a skull, which is called in the Hebrew Golgotha: Where they crucified Him, and two other with Him, on either side one, and Jesus in the midst. And Pilate wrote a title, and put it on the cross. And the writing was, JESUS OF NAZARETH THE KING OF THE JEWS" (John 19:17–19).

"After this, Jesus knowing that all things were now accomplished, that the Scripture might be fulfilled, saith, I thirst. Now there was set a vessel full of vinegar: and they filled a spunge with vinegar, and put it upon hyssop, and put it to His mouth. When Jesus therefore had received the vinegar, He said, *It is finished*: and He bowed His head, and gave up the ghost.

"The Jews therefore, because it was the preparation, that the bodies should not remain upon the cross on the sabbath day, (for that sabbath day was an high day,) besought Pilate that their legs might be broken, and that they might be taken away. Then came the soldiers, and brake the legs of the first, and of the other which was crucified with Him. But when they came to Jesus, and saw that He was dead already, they brake not His legs: But one of the soldiers with a spear pierced His side, and forthwith came there out blood and water.

"And he that saw it bare record, and his record is true: and he knoweth that he saith true, that ye might believe. For these things were done, that the Scripture should be fulfilled, A bone of Him shall not be broken. And again another Scripture saith, They shall look on Him whom they pierced.

"And after this Joseph of Arimathaea, being a disciple of Jesus, but secretly for fear of the Jews, besought Pilate that he might take away the body of Jesus: and Pilate gave him leave. He came therefore, and took the body of Jesus. And there came also Nicodemus, which at the first came to Jesus by night, and brought a mixture of myrrh and aloes, about an hundred pound weight. Then took they the body of Jesus, and wound it in linen clothes with the spices, as the manner of the Jews is to bury. Now in the place where He was crucified there was a garden; and in the garden a new sepulchre, wherein was never man yet laid. There laid they Jesus therefore because of the Jews' preparation day; for the sepulchre was nigh at hand" (John 19:28—42).

In these verses John the Beloved tells of the fulfillment of prophecy — Jesus was crucified, they pierced His hands and His feet, they cast lots for His garments, not a bone of Him was broken — and He was laid in Joseph's tomb. But death could not hold Him. John 20:1—20 tells of *further fulfillment* of David's prophecy:

"The first day of the week cometh Mary Magdalene early, when it was yet dark, unto the sepulchre, and seeth the stone taken away from the sepulchre. Then she runneth, and cometh to Simon Peter, and to the other disciple, whom Jesus loved, and saith unto them, They have taken away the Lord out of the sepulchre, and we know not where they have laid Him.

"Peter therefore went forth, and that other disciple, and came to the sepulchre. So they ran both together: and the other disciple did outrun Peter, and came first to the sepulchre. And he stooping down, and looking in, saw the linen clothes lying; yet went he not in. Then cometh Simon Peter following him, and went into the sepulchre, and seeth the linen clothes lie, and the napkin, that was about His head, not lying with the linen clothes, but wrapped together in a place by itself. Then went in also that other disciple, which came first to the sepulchre, and he saw, and believed. For as yet they knew not the Scripture, that He must rise again from the dead.

"Then the disciples went away again unto their own home. But Mary stood without at the sepulchre weeping: and as she wept, she stooped down, and looked into the sepulchre, and seeth two angels in white sitting, the one at the head, and the other at the feet, where the body of Jesus had lain. And they say unto her, Woman, why weepest thou? She saith unto them, Because they have taken away my Lord, and I know not where they have laid Him. And when she had thus said, she turned herself back, and saw Jesus standing, and knew not that it was Jesus.

"Jesus saith unto her, Woman, why weepest thou? whom seekest thou? She, supposing Him to be the gardener, saith unto Him, Sir, if thou have borne Him hence, tell me where thou hast laid Him, and I will take Him away. Jesus saith unto her, Mary. She turned herself, and saith unto Him, Rabboni; which is to say, Master. Jesus saith unto her, Touch me not; for I am not yet ascended to my Father: but go to my brethren, and say unto them, I ascend unto my Father, and your Father; and to my God, and your God. Mary Magdalene came and told the disciples that she had seen the Lord, and that He had spoken these things unto her.

"Then the same day at evening, being the first day of the week, when the doors were shut where the disciples were assembled for fear of the Jews, came Jesus and stood in the midst, and saith unto them, Peace be unto you. And when He had so said, He shewed unto them His hands and His side. Then were the disciples glad, when they

167

saw the Lord."

Thus was prophecy fulfilled. Death could not hold Him, His flesh did not see corruption. He was crucified in a body like unto our body, sin apart; He was raised in a glorified body, a body incorruptible; and one day we who are born again will have a body just like the glorified body of Jesus: ". . . we know that, when He shall appear, *we shall be like Him*; for we shall see Him as He is" (I John 3:2).

His death was prophesied by David centuries before it happened. He was pierced as prophesied, and "not a bone of Him was broken." Death could not hold Him, and He rose again bodily as prophesied. The Scriptures cannot be broken. The Word of God is just as up-to-date as tomorrow's morning headlines in our newspapers.

XI

To *Isaiah* was revealed God's part in the death of the Lord Jesus Christ, and to him God revealed that Christ would be identified with transgressors, that He would pray for them, and that He would "make His grave with the rich." (He was buried in a rich man's tomb—the tomb of Joseph of Arimathaea.) More than seven centuries before it happened, God spoke to Isaiah and he penned down these words:

"Who hath believed our report? and to whom is the arm of the Lord revealed? For He shall grow up before Him as a tender plant, and as a root out of a dry ground: He hath no form nor comeliness; and when we shall see Him, there is no beauty that we should desire Him.

"He is despised and rejected of men; a man of sorrows, and acquainted with grief: and we hid as it were our faces from Him; He was despised, and we esteemed Him not. *Surely He hath borne our griefs, and carried our sorrows: yet we did esteem Him stricken, SMITTEN OF*

GOD, and afflicted. But He was wounded for OUR transgressions, He was bruised for OUR iniquities: the chastisement of OUR peace was upon Him; and with His stripes WE are healed.

"All we like sheep have gone astray; we have turned every one to his own way; and the Lord hath laid on Him the iniquity of us all. He was oppressed, and He was afflicted, yet He opened not His mouth: He is brought as a lamb to the slaughter, and as a sheep before her shearers is dumb, so He openeth not His mouth.

"He was taken from prison and from judgment: and who shall declare His generation? for He was cut off out of the land of the living: for the transgression of my people was He stricken. And He made His grave with the wicked, and with the rich in His death; because He had done no violence, neither was any deceit in His mouth.

"Yet it pleased the Lord to bruise Him; He hath put Him to grief: when thou shalt make His soul an offering for sin, He shall see His seed, He shall prolong His days, and the pleasure of the Lord shall prosper in His hand. He shall see of the travail of His soul, and shall be satisfied: by His knowledge shall my righteous servant justify many; for He shall bear their iniquities. Therefore will I divide Him a portion with the great, and He shall divide the spoil with the strong; because He hath poured out His soul unto death: and He was numbered with the transgressors; and He bare the sin of many, and made intercession for the transgressors" (Isa. 53:1–12).

Beloved, the Lord Jesus Christ who paid our sin-debt was "smitten of God." What do we mean by that? We simply mean that wicked men did not take His life, He laid it down: "Therefore doth my Father love me, because I lay down my life, that I might take it again. No man taketh it from me, BUT I LAY IT DOWN OF MYSELF. I have the power to lay it down, and I have power to take it again. THIS COMMANDMENT HAVE I RECEIVED OF MY FATHER" (John 10:17,18).

Jesus literally passed His life back to the heavenly

Father. At the appointed time—*the very split second*—the Lamb of God was to die, *He DIED*. God smote Him -- and even though we may not understand this, we must accept it as fact. If *God* had not smitten Jesus, the *cross* would not have killed Him. If His death had been dependent upon the nails in His hands and the spikes in His feet, He would still be hanging on the cross today waiting for death, because NO MAN could take His life. He was God in flesh, and He took a body a little lower than the angels in order that He might die, that He might taste death for every man (Heb. 2:9). It is true that His own nation demanded His death and wicked men drove the nails through His hands and His feet; but unless we deny the Word of God we must confess that the sacrificial Lamb was *"smitten of God."*

"And Jesus cried with a loud voice, and gave up the ghost. And the veil of the temple was rent in twain from the top to the bottom. And when the centurion, which stood over against Him, saw that He so cried out, and gave up the ghost, he said, TRULY THIS MAN WAS THE SON OF GOD" (Mark 15:37–39).

No doubt this centurion had seen many men die – but he had never witnessed a death such as this! Jesus cried *"with a LOUD voice"*—not the voice of a dying man, but a thunderous cry of victory—and literally gave His life into the hands of God. No wonder the centurion exclaimed, "Truly THIS MAN was the Son of God!"

Why Should God Say More?

The Bible is an open book. Bibles can be purchased for pennies today. Most people can read, and those who cannot read have loved ones or friends who can read to them; and since God has clearly prophesied about Jesus, and each of these prophecies to date has been literally fulfilled, would sinners believe if God added another book

170

to the sixty-six books already given?

Briefly summarizing what we have covered in this message, we found that centuries before Christ was born, God revealed to Adam that the Saviour would be the seed of the woman (Gen. 3:15). The apostles in the New Testament declare that He WAS the seed of the woman, born of a virgin.

To Abraham God revealed the nation with which Jesus would be identified. He was definitely identified with the nation Israel.

To Jacob God made known the fact that Jesus would be of the tribe of Judah. He *was* born of the Jews. His mother Mary gave Him His flesh, God gave Him His blood.

To David God revealed that Jesus would be of his family, that He would sit on the throne of David. The first part of this prophecy has already been fulfilled, and the last part of it *will be* fulfilled in God's own time.

To Daniel God unfolded the *time* that Jesus would appear, and it came to pass exactly as prophesied.

To Micah it was clearly revealed that He would be born in Bethlehem. This was fulfilled as prophesied and is clearly borne out in the Gospels.

To Malachi the Holy Spirit revealed that the Saviour would be preceded by a forerunner, one who would announce His coming. John the Baptist was that one.

To Zechariah the Holy Spirit revealed that Jesus would be sold for thirty pieces of silver, and that He would ride into Jerusalem on a little donkey. Judas Iscariot bargained with the scribes and Pharisees to betray Him for *thirty pieces of silver*! He DID ride into Jerusalem on a donkey, and Judas DID betray Him for the price of a slave.

To the Psalmist God made known the manner of the death of Jesus, that not one bone of His body would be broken, and that death could not hold Him. He *did* die by crucifixion as prophesied, none of His bones were broken, and He *rose from the dead* as prophesied.

To Isaiah it was revealed that Christ would be smitten of God, that He would be identified with transgressors, and that He would bear the sins of the whole wide world. He was crucified between two thieves, nailing our sins to His cross, and "whosoever" will accept His finished work will be saved.

With these prophecies and their fulfillment written down in God's holy Word for us, why should He speak any more? It is not necessary that He add to that which is already perfect. We have the perfect law of liberty, we have all of the Scriptures inspired of God, and the man of God is perfectly and thoroughly furnished with all he needs in order to preach salvation, instruct believers in the victorious Christian walk, and himself live as a Christian should.

Sinner friend, if you do not believe what has already been written in God's Word, you would not believe if Jesus Christ Himself should come to earth today and walk the streets of your city, preaching in person! The Bible is the Word of God, the *living Word*, the Word that brings light and life if you will only believe it.

In Closing

Jesus said, "Verily, verily, I say unto you, *He that heareth my Word, and believeth on Him that sent me, hath everlasting life*, and shall not come into condemnation; but is passed from death unto life" (John 5:24).

What IS His Word? "*For God so loved the world, that*

172

He gave His only begotten Son, that whosoever believeth in Him should not perish, but have everlasting life. For God sent not His Son into the world to condemn the world; but that the world through Him might be saved. He that believeth on Him is NOT condemned: but he that believeth not is condemned ALREADY, because he hath not believed in the name of the only begotten Son of God" (John 3: 16—18).

There is enough Gospel in those three verses to save the whole wide world if the world would hear and believe it! Jesus left the bosom of the Father and came to man's abode. He took upon Himself a body, He humbled Himself and became obedient unto death—even the death of the cross; *but before He died He FINISHED the work the Father sent Him to do.* He announced God's love, He made plain the way of salvation. He taught in the streets, in the synagogues, from the mountains – and He proved His ministry by the things He did. Nicodemus declared, "No man can do these miracles that thou doest, except God be with him" (John 3:2). Even the officers who were sent on one occasion to arrest Him declared, *"Never man spake like this Man"* (John 7:46). Why? Jesus gave the answer in John 6:63: "It is the Spirit that quickeneth; the flesh profiteth nothing: *the WORDS that I speak unto you, they are spirit, and they are life."*

Dear reader, if you have read thus far in this message, you have been exposed to the Word of God. It could be that you have never had an *opportunity* to be saved. It could be that you have never had anyone sit down and *explain the plan of salvation* to you. It may be that up to this very hour you have had some excuse for not being a Christian, but from this time forward you are inexcusable! In this message you have been given the Word of God, and the Word of God brings salvation. The Word of God tells us that God loves us, Jesus died for us, and that we are saved by grace through faith in His finished work. The Word of God tells us that salvation is free—*the gift of God*; and anyone knows that the only way to come into possession of a gift is to receive it from the giver. *God* so loved you that He gave Jesus to die for you; *Jesus* so loved you that He came into the world and laid down His *life* that you might be saved; and all He asks you to do is HEAR His Word and believe on the only begotten Son of God who died for your sins. If you will do that, God will save you. He promised—and He cannot lie (Heb. 6:18; Tit. 1:2).

If you are an unbeliever, get a Bible *now*. If you do not have one, go *buy* one. If you cannot buy one, go *borrow* one. Then turn to John's Gospel and read John 1:12,13; 3:16–18; 5:24. Then read John 6:37 and hear Jesus say, "Him that cometh to me I will in no wise cast out."

I have given you the Word of God in this message, and if you refuse to HEAR it, then you stand to be *judged* by the very Word you refuse to hear! (John 12:47,48).

Believer, bow your head and thank God that you heard the Word, believed and received the Word. Thank God that you are saved; worship Him and thank Him for His mercies to you.

Sinner, hear the words of Paul and Silas: "Believe on the Lord Jesus Christ, and thou shalt be saved" (Acts 16:31). Bow your head and in your own words confess to God that you are a sinner, that you believe He loved you and sent Jesus to die for you. Confess to Him that you believe Jesus was born of the virgin, that He died on the cross for your sins, that He was buried and raised the third day according to the Scriptures. Ask God to save you for Jesus' sake—and He will do it. He will save you—and you will know it!

In closing let me give you the verse that transformed me from a miserable sinner to a child of God:

"If thou shalt confess with thy mouth the Lord Jesus, and shalt believe in thine heart that God hath raised Him from the dead, thou shalt be saved" (Rom. 10:9).